SIGNALS

SIGNALS

An Inspiring Story of Life After Life

Joel Rothschild

NEW WORLD LIBRARY
NOVATO, CALIFORNIA

New World Library
14 Pamaron Way
Novato, CA 94949

© 2000, 2001 Joel Michael Rothschild

Editing: Katherine Dieter, Marc Allen
Cover and text design: Mary Ann Casler

Library of Congress Cataloging-in-Publication Data
Rothschild, Joel, 1957–
Signals : a true story of life after life / Joel Rothschild.
p.   cm.
ISBN 1-57731-179-5 (paperback : alk. paper)
ISBN 1-57731-150-7 (hardcover : alk. paper)
1. Future life — Case studies. 2. Rothschild, Joel, 1957– I. Title.

BF1311.F8 R68 2000   99-049354
133.9'01'3 — dc21   CIP

First paperback printing, March 2001
ISBN 1-57731-179-5
Printed in Canada on acid-free paper
Distributed to the trade by Publishers Group West

10 9 8 7 6 5 4 3 2 1

*"The best portion of a good man's life
is his little nameless unremembered acts
of kindness and love."*

— William Wordsworth

This Book Is Dedicated

To Sharon Shaw — without her love and support I would
not have lived to have experienced the miracles
chronicled on these pages.

To my family for their own special love,
and especially my sister Patti Ward,
who has dedicated her life to underprivileged children.

To Philip Rothschild, who has dealt with
AIDS as long as myself.

To my friends Gary Goldberg, Monty Hill, David Raff,
Johnathon Kanes, Katie Haber, Rita Wainer,
David Hockney, Pat Gregor, David Bay-Andersen,
Bill Brown, and all those other friends mentioned
in this book with whom I've been blessed
to share laughter, love, and warmth.

To Billy Bologna and Mark Simon's entire family
and the countless others who took care of the dying
during the worst of this crisis.

To Marc Allen, Katherine Dieter, Jeff Indusi, Jeff
Yarbrough, and Lee Gurst for seeing merit in my story.

Contents

Publisher's Preface

A s soon as I read the first few pages of this manuscript, I was certain that every word of it was true. After I met Joel Rothschild, I was absolutely convinced.

A hummingbird mysteriously appears to Joel several times throughout the events he describes. It has landed on his shoulder, and allowed him to hold it in his hand, even hand it to a friend. If this were a work of fiction, it would be labeled magical realism.

Katherine Dieter, a fine writer and editor, helped polish Joel's manuscript, and she told me a hummingbird kept appearing and watching as she worked. I did a final edit myself, and the first time I took a break from it and wandered outside, a hummingbird appeared and hovered about ten inches in front of my face for several seconds. This has never happened before, or since. He seemed to be checking me out with a critical eye. He seemed to be saying, "Who is this guy? Is he good enough to work on this book?"

He stared directly into my eyes, and then seemed

to say, "Get back to work! This book is important!"

Maybe I'm just imagining things. But the things Joel has experienced are far more substantial — they're miraculous, in fact, and wonderful. This is undoubtedly an important book, one that has the power to change some of our old beliefs, and to considerably lighten our lives.

Marc Allen, Publisher
Novato, California

Foreword

By Neale Donald Walsch

I was gazing last night at the bridges of Florence. They are beautiful during the daytime, but even more breathtaking at night. With their sparkling lights and stately majesty, they bring a special magic to this very special city in Italy, and as I looked upon them last night, strolling in the gentle breezes of the Piazzale Michelangelo above the city, I was struck with a powerful metaphor.

Bridges are the most important part of our life.

I think Albert may have sent me that thought.

Who is Albert? Ah, that is something for you to find out, right here, in this remarkable book. I didn't know anything about Albert until I got back to my hotel room after last evening's drive to the *piazzala*. I'd been carrying Joel Rothschild's book, *Signals*, around with me for days, through Korea, through Oslo, and through half of Italy, as I journeyed forth through a world tour to carry to people around the globe the message of *Conversations with God,* which, in beautiful summation, is simply, we are all one. As I met people of differing cultures and traditions, of differing languages and backgrounds and beliefs, I pondered each day, more and more as the trip went on: How can we get this idea of Oneness across to all humans everywhere? How can I close the gap that separates us, leaving us each marooned on our own shore?

Then I stood last night above the city of Florence, saw the reflection of the bridges on the waters of the Fiumo Arno, and I received my gift of insight.

When I awoke this morning, I felt an urgent need to read Joel's manuscript. Not a bit of a need, not a medium-sized need — an urgent need. So I plunged into it. The tour of the Galleria dell'Accademia, the viewing of the original *David*, would have to wait. There was something else — some other art, some other gift of inestimable beauty — I was to receive this day.

I have received that gift, and now I pass it on to you. If you are reading this, you are holding it in your hands. Do not put it down. Do not return it to the shelf, or to the table, or to the place whence it came. Take it home with you. You are meant to have this gift, or you would not have found a way to bring it to you. Now all that is left is for you to be willing to receive it.

This book is a bridge. It is a bridge between worlds, and a bridge between the worlds we create within this world. And this bridge could make a world of difference. For it will bridge the gap for many, between what they know, and what they think they know, and what is really so, about all the world — and the world after this world.

This is a book about life and death and love and God and, well, just all of it. It was written by a gay man, and it therefore holds the gay experience on its pages. Whether you are gay or straight, I believe you will experience this book as a great bridge for all of us. I have been looking for such a bridge for a very long time, and especially since the *Conversations with God* dialogue, which made it explicitly clear that God embraces homosexuals in His eternal and everlasting love, just as He embraces all of us. I have been searching, ever since then, for a way to carry this message to all the world, and to that part of the world which is gay, that we might heal the divisions between us — between all of us...not just gays and straights, but blacks and whites, Christians and Jews, Muslims and Eastern Orthodox Christians, Irish Catholics and Protestants, men and women, and any of the other artificial separations that we have created between us.

I've found that bridge here, in a beautiful book that closes the greatest gap of all — the gulf in our understandings of Life and Death — as well. Do I agree with everything is this book? Every inference, every nuance, every shade of meaning? No. Perhaps that is a sign of my limited ability to totally comprehend, or maybe it's just a healthy indication of my continuing unwillingness to close myself to all the questions. I want to leave some more things open for me to yet discover. Yet I find the largest portion of what is written here more than merely inspiring. I find it illuminating — a revelation of enormous impact and importance.

Still, I must tell you that there is one statement in Joel's book with which I totally disagree. It is just the fourth sentence of the book. That sentence reads, "As human beings, we are all quite limited in our ability to understand each other's experience." Joel himself — with the eloquence of his writing, the depth of his insight, the openness and the honesty and the courage of his sharing, and the absolute purity of his intent — has turned that statement into a lie. I understand his experience completely. So, too, will you. For he has spoken here with a voice that resides in all of us, and has thus given voice to the part of each of us which yearns to be heard. It is that part of us that knows of love, and that seeks to express and experience that love unconditionally, and eternally. This is something we all understand, this is something we all hold in common, this is that which transcends our petty and shallow and cosmetic differences, and binds us together in oneness.

You do not need to be gay to understand this book, or the people in it. You merely need to be human, and to be in touch with your humanity. Yet the beauty of this book is that its effect is circular — it will put you in touch with your humanity, even if you were not there at the outset. And then it will do something more. It will put you in touch with the part of yourself that is greater than your humanity. It will cause you to see Who You Really Are.

This book answers your life's greatest question. It allows you to know that answer before your death, which will be your life's greatest gift. And so, this book is that Treasure of Treasures for which every thinking person searches. It is a source of eternal truth. It contains what I call Becalming Wisdom, allowing the mind to rest at last in sure and certain knowledge that what our own soul has been telling us from the beginning has been true. We have been waiting for a long time for such a signal. Now, here again, God sends it to us. In yet another form. Through yet another voice. At yet another time.

Thank you, Joel, for speaking with courage and wisdom and love.

Neale Donald Walsch
September 3, 1999
Florence, Italy

Acknowledgments

A very special thanks to my friend, Dr. Keith Del Villar. He is a research molecular biologist, and works long hours for little pay, as do most scientists. His research is very demanding, and he has sacrificed most of the very little free time he has to help me with this book. The research scientists of our country are an army of tireless heroes, and they receive little praise. These heroes have developed the drugs and made the medical advances that have in part kept me alive. Their dedicated, brilliant work has saved millions of lives.

Keith is currently researching a gene that triggers pancreatic cancer. This work will advance science another step closer to a cure. He will soon leave that research to begin work on Alzheimer's disease. Like all scientists, he works in cooperation with many other scientists. No breakthrough or advance has been a solo endeavor. The miracles of science are built on the work of the past. It is sweat and perseverance that triumphs over disease. Knowing Keith, I have a deeper appreciation for the dedication involved in the development of AIDS drugs.

I would also like to thank two other friends: Elizabeth Taylor and Keith Haring. Elizabeth stepped up to bat when no one was present. She used her celebrity status to fund research, inform others, and fight discrimination. She single-handedly changed the face of AIDS and saved countless lives. Her generous work, dedication, personal sacrifices, and gifts of time and money have been enormous. I hope history will remember this as much as it remembers her acting career.

Keith Haring funded numerous charities. He was there with substantial contributions when groups like ACT UP needed it. His money allowed political activists to change the way pending drugs are studied on humans. These activists changed our FDA and made it possible for terminally ill patients to obtain foreign treatments and promising drugs faster. At a time when all studies were required to be double-blind, they helped develop compassionate-use and expanded-access drug studies. This work got promising drugs to the dying years faster and extended countless lives. These changes in an antiquated system may have come because of AIDS. It is heartening to think that something positive has come out of this disease. These changes will benefit millions of people with other diseases now and in the future. AIDS research has advanced science in ways unimaginable just a few years ago. Keith died in 1989; I hope the world will remember his acts of kindness and generosity.

Introduction

Sharon Shaw was the first person I truly loved and trusted. She gave me the courage to go on and fight when I was dying with AIDS. Up until 1995, I never believed I would live long enough to write this book.

In 1986, my physicians gave me less than three years to live. In 1994, they predicted my death in less than twelve months. It is now 1999 and I am alive and healthy. I have outlived my doctors' prognosis. I have even outlived two of my doctors. These are good days for me. I have been given a second lease on life. That, however, is only part of the story. This story is about a far greater miracle that occurred in my life.

A few years back, I sat down to write Sharon a letter. It's so hard to imagine that I could drift away from someone so significant in my life. We used to speak every day, and see each other more than once a week. In the past few years, I've seen her only briefly. It is not that we don't still deeply love each other, but life ebbs and flows and takes even the closest of friends in new and different directions.

I sat down to write her a note, and that note became this book. As I wrote it, my thoughts kept wandering back to the same theme: how life always changes, especially in unexpected ways. Being alive is an unexpected change in my life. I am now one of the longest-living AIDS survivors. Yet even that is not the most unexpected change in my life. This is not just my survivor's tale. It is the story of a spiritual and psychic awakening that was thrust upon me.

This story is completely true. I write focused on the facts. I've tried to skip personal sentiment when it was not critical to the story. I am reminded of Viktor Frankl's story of the Holocaust in his historic book *Man's Search for Meaning,* though I dare not compare our experiences or books, knowing how profoundly moving his experiences were. Once, I heard him speak. He said he originally wanted his book published anonymously. He felt the things he wrote about were more significant than his own life, that his commentary meant nothing, and that the factual documentation of his experience was all that mattered. I have always admired his book, and I feel exactly the same way. I believe that the events that began on June 1, 1994, and culminated in the publication of this book are bigger and more significant than my own life. I am unable to separate my personal history from those events. My experiences with AIDS are entwined with the psychic events documented in this book. I am very much a skeptic by nature, but the experiences in this book have eroded my skepticism.

On *Star Trek,* they had the Vulcan Mind Probe, and in Natalie Wood's final film, *Brainstorm,* they had a device to transfer the feelings and experiences of one person to another, a device that allowed one to live exactly what another has lived. If only these things were available to me in sharing this story. It's a wonderful fantasy, but in real life it is impossible to fully understand someone else's experience. So much of what we learn must be experienced first-hand in order for us to accept it. Our communication is limited. It seems especially difficult to explain suffering to those who do not know its face. It's even harder to explain abstract and highly personal notions like healing, growth, and hope. It seems nearly impossible to explain metaphysical encounters and signals from beyond.

Before these events, I would dismiss similar stories as fantasies concocted by the writer. I'm sure you will question these events, as well. My life was drastically altered by them. My sense of peace, resolve, and acceptance has grown considerably because of the events outlined in this book. My health has rebounded further and faster, undoubtedly helped by a new outlook on life and death, as well as by new AIDS drugs. Previously, AIDS had diminished my natural denial of my own death, but it hadn't diminished my skepticism of an afterlife. Yet that skepticism has now dissolved, almost completely, because of a series of miraculous signals from beyond. I have come to see that there is far more in heaven and earth than I had dreamt of in my old agnostic philosophy. It is my deepest hope that this book may help someone to find a light at the end of even the darkest tunnel. Perhaps together we can focus on the glass being half full when it appears half empty. In my life, broken dreams and shattered plans have, with the help of time, become fertile ground for new flowers, new experiences and creations that I couldn't have imagined a few years ago — like this book, for example.

CHAPTER 1

A Life Taken, A Promise Broken

June 1, 1994

Hatred has been built and sustained on generalizations, and therefore I distrust generalizations. There is some truth, however, to the fact that we relate more easily to those most similar to ourselves, and often find it harder to understand those different from ourselves. Perhaps it is true that white people cannot fully understand the black experience, nor can Christians fully understand Jews, men fully understand women, gays fully understand straights, and so on.

As human beings, we are all quite limited in our ability to understand each other's experience. We all possess varying degrees of empathy and sensitivity. Those with the gift of great empathy and sensitivity carry a huge burden in this life. My friend Albert possessed more than any person I have ever met. Albert could not kill an insect without thinking of its death. He was a vegetarian because eating flesh would be to consume that animal's pain at death.

It is not easy for me to try to convey my feelings to you, armed with only ink and paper. I want to express what I felt at noon on June 1, 1994, when I opened the door and crossed the threshold of Albert's little home to find him dead. The room was filled with spent candles; a single votive was still burning. An empty wine bottle sat on the table, the shades were drawn, and the floor was strewn with empty pill capsules.

My greatest friend, my ally, my family, my life, my joy, my laughter, had taken his own life. No words, no eloquent description of how I wept holding his cold, gray body will ever convey the shock, rage, and agony in every cell of my body. I felt sick. My heart raced and pounded, my ears rang. I cried out, "Why? No Albert, not you!" I thought this must be a dream. Lord, make me wake up. Please God, let me wake up from this nightmare.

But I knew full well it was no dream, and I cried and rocked and held the cold flesh of the best friend I had ever known. I was shivering — something inside my body was fighting the shock. I struggled not to faint, not to vomit or collapse. He had taken his own life. That selfish act had broken every promise he had ever made to me, including the promise he would never abandon me.

We had talked about suicide. What had we not

talked about in all those years of friendship? We had both agreed that if either one of us ever took his own life, we would say a good-bye, and give each other at least twenty-four-hours notice. We would spend that final time together ... I wanted my goddamn twenty-four hours!

Albert had not called. Perhaps after twenty-four hours together, he would have changed his mind. He would not have done it. Didn't he know how much I loved him? I must have told him a million times. I know I told him another million times how much he meant to me. I was angry, shaking with rage. He had betrayed me. I searched for a note, an explanation. There was none. I cried out to Albert and God, "Why? Why?"

The pain got worse. It was volcanic, exploding from within my heart. I didn't know how I would make it through the next minute, let alone an hour, or a day. I screamed out, "You fucking bastard! I meant nothing to you! How could you do this to me? How could you leave me here all alone? Why now? You never loved me!"

We had discussed death. We had both been diagnosed HIV-positive for many years, and both of us had lost many friends. I had been extremely ill for years, and was actually contemplating my own suicide at the time. Albert was the one in absolutely perfect health. Albert was the optimist, the spiritual one, with a belief in an afterlife. We had long ago promised that whoever was first to die would try to contact the other — with a signal, with whatever psychic ability he might have. He would signal that there was a world beyond. This would be our signal of hope.

Now, I couldn't care less about this pact. I didn't want his signals. Nothing he could do from beyond would matter. If he wrote my name across the sky with a rainbow, or gave me mystical powers, I wouldn't care. Whatever he did wouldn't be as real as flesh and blood and friendship. It would never matter. He had broken our promise and abandoned me. I would never hear his voice again. It was the only time he ever lied to me — and it was the greatest lie imaginable. He was gone. The body I held would never move again. I needed to know now that he loved me while he was alive, that everything we shared was real, and he could not tell me that.

The coroner, the sheriff, and friends arrived, and they pried my hands off his corpse. I couldn't leave the room. They finally left me alone, crying and screaming. I could hear them outside. Someone said, "Leave him alone for a while." And someone else said, "For God's sake, take him home." I vowed never to leave that spot. I would never move again.

All I could feel was pain. I lost all track of time. Minutes seemed like hours.

His body was taken away. I knew I would never feel his flesh again. I would never hear his voice again. I sat in despair, almost frozen for an unknown amount of time.

The noise of people outside calmed down. The police had gone and only a few friends remained, waiting for me to exit. They were there to support me on my way home. They were quiet. I was only whimpering now; I'd stopped screaming. The light of day started to fade, and I began to feel an eerie calm. It lasted only a short while, but felt strangely soothing. Then I felt his presence, as if he were speaking. I did not hear words with my ears, but I sensed a faint cry that no sensory organ could register. I *felt* his voice. He was pleading with me, telling me to go outside behind the house next door where I would find a trash can.

You will find the note that you need. Get that note, then go home.

I ran outside to the trash can behind the house next door, frantically searching through garbage and waste. Everyone thought I had gone mad. There, at the very bottom, I found Albert's last written words.

He had buried the note in the neighbors' garbage so it would never be found. The note was not even completed. Words throughout had been scratched off. It was covered with impressions of teardrops. The crumpled letter began, "To my most dear love Joel," and ended, "You are my dearest friend. I shall always love you." That was exactly what I needed to know. I needed to know that I was in his final thoughts.

I was less betrayed, and that little note carried me home. I retreated to the comfort of my own bed. It was a haven from the emptiness of the outside world, and I even found a bit of joy in the knowledge that we had indeed shared an everlasting friendship.

Later that night, Albert came to me again, and then again in the days and months that followed. Time would have to pass before I could realize he had given me an incredible gift. At that point in my life, I had no way of knowing how my future would be altered. How could I have known that a ripple effect would impact the lives of so many others? How could I have known that I would go from the depths of despair to a life of gratitude, even joy, and my childhood prayers would be answered, and my life would find new meaning?

These profound changes are hard for me to sketch with words. I worry that ink on paper will reduce the majesty of the moments that have passed.

Explaining the ride will never quite equal the sensation of living it. All that aside, let me attempt it.

CHAPTER 2

A Brief History, A List of Names

Albert's suicide came at the worst of times. Three other close friends were dying, my own health was failing, and I had just barely gotten over an opportunistic infection. My life had always been a roller-coaster ride of twists and turns; perhaps everyone's life is like that. His death showed me that the unexpected would become commonplace. I had been certain Albert would outlive me. A friend once said, "It's never the script you expected it to be." Those words had become all too real.

June 1, 1994, would alter the course of my life forever. It started out as a morning much like any other morning. I guess many dramatic, life-altering events begin with ordinary mornings. I was feeling rather well, which in itself was a bit of a miracle. My health had been deteriorating over the previous year. I had been struggling to stay alive for several months, and had been losing weight and feeling weak more often than not. Albert was my support structure. He was my safety net.

Albert's was the dearest and most loving friendship of my life. Who can explain why great friendships evolve, or even why people fall in love? I am not sure what part chemistry, timing, or destiny plays in these affairs of the heart. I am certain that trust, respect, and admiration were essential to our relationship.

Our relationship was different from anything I had ever known, because Albert was different from anyone I had ever known. He was extremely gentle, even kind to a fault. He often gave others money at the expense of his own eating or paying rent. He volunteered at AIDS hospices even though doing so made it much more difficult for him to deal with his own depression and fears about his future.

Albert was baffled by this world, and sometimes looked like a deer caught in headlights. He was very handsome, so much so that men and women were always making advances. One day he quite seriously told me that great beauty was a burden. I thought he was being sarcastic. I had never been a great beauty and had no idea what that statement meant. Later I came to realize that physically attractive people often have to reject suitors and, for Albert, causing any pain to others was intensely difficult. I think this played a part in his suicide.

Albert never realized his full potential. He was a brilliant artist and photographer. His talent was well beyond that of a great many others who have found fame and fortune. He had an enormous flair for design, and great style. He could ignite any room he entered, always in a quiet, subtle manner. We enjoyed a close friendship for many years. It was a strange and serendipitous relationship.

We were both raised in Miami. I grew up in Miami Beach and was the only son in a Jewish family that was, unfortunately, a typical dysfunctional family. I went to a conservative Hebrew school until my bar mitzvah. After that, I had no religious contact with the synagogue, or any sense of spirituality. The strict tenets of the Jewish faith did not appeal to me, and I became an agnostic.

My greatest joy growing up was the ocean. That was my haven and escape as a child. We lived on the water at a time before pollution and dredging destroyed the natural ecosystem. I spent countless days alone, scuba diving and exploring the reefs just beyond our backyard.

Albert was the only son of a Cuban doctor. He lived in the Hialeah section of Miami. His upbringing was strict and Catholic. We were both from small families; we each had one sister. To our parents' dismay, neither one of us would propagate our family name. Our families were not equipped to handle a gay child — but then, perhaps no family is really prepared for that experience.

Albert's haven and escape was dance. Our worlds gently collided in 1977 on the dance floor of Uncle Charlie's Disco, in Miami. Gloria Gaynor was singing "I Will Survive," and Albert was practicing his dance moves for an appearance on the TV show *Dance Fever.* The only thing we had in common was that we were both too young to be in the club, both out of the closet, and both should have been home studying.

We spoke most Saturday nights for the better part of two years. We would talk about how everyone else in the club was older and different from us. We talked about music, and we danced. I would compliment Albert on his dance moves and attire. He would compliment me on my physique. They were shallow conversations. It was the seventies and we were teenagers, two kids in an adult's world. This casual relationship never became much more than that. I left Miami for college, and Albert finished high school and left for New York City to become a model. We saw each other a few times in New York, but then were separated for over a decade.

I earned my college degree, and grew up in the process. I opened a business, a gym and health spa in Atlanta. After a few successful years, the epidemic struck, and I watched countless customers get sick and die. There were so many that, by 1984, a thriving business that once had thousands of members was struggling to survive. Many of the customers not infected with AIDS reentered the closet. Others seemed to recoil into their antebellum homes, isolating with cats or dogs as their sole comfort. The gay community in Atlanta was shrinking.

I decided to pack my bags for sunnier weather, and move to Los Angeles. I figured that since the gay population was exponentially larger in L.A., the impact of AIDS wouldn't be quite as devastating as it was in Atlanta. I would be free to pursue the adventures of life and dating.

I settled in quite nicely. I had acquired a tidy sum from the gym in Georgia, and my bodybuilder physique assured me a welcome reception. In a short time, I had a new partner named Mark Simon, and a wonderful small circle of close friends. I was productive, working hard, and I enjoyed the sunshine.

This somewhat typical, hedonistic California lifestyle continued for a few years, which to a younger person seems like a long time. It was long enough to get comfortable in plans for the future, but my plans were suddenly shattered. One bright, sunny day I had some slight trouble breathing, a sore throat, and small swollen lymph nodes in my neck. I ignored these symptoms for a few days, and then began to run a fever that raged to 104 degrees. It forced me to consult a physician. After years of what I thought was safe sex, I was diagnosed with a lung infection related to AIDS.

I spent the next few years in and out of hospitals, doctors' offices, and support groups, fighting for my health. Most of the time, it felt like putting air into a leaky tire. I struggled my best to preserve my health, my relationships, and thoughts of a future, but it was not easy. I kept myself glued together enough to function, but my life moved at a much slower pace. Although a cylinder or two short, it still ran with some efficiency. I still worked out regularly, and enjoyed the company of my small group of friends. Even though my health declined, I was unusually lucky from 1984 to 1992. Only one close friend died during that time. The word "friend" has come to mean something very special to me. There are many tiers or levels to our relationships, and some people we call friends are not as close as others. Several people, whom I knew and respected and admired, were dying.

The one close friend who died during that time was Robert Cohen. We had shared a long, joyous history. I remembered talking to Robert years before about my garden in Atlanta, and mentioning how beautiful it had become with the years that passed.

Robert said, "You know, Joel, gardens are about time." I agreed, and said, "So are friendships."

The passing of time can be a marvelous thing. Plants grow and blossom, friendships deepen, and grief softens only with time.

Somehow, I learned to block out the grief and loss of those less close to me. It was my way of surviving, and it worked well until one afternoon when I picked up my old address book and looked for a telephone number, and began to count how many people in the book were dead. I had notes in my phone book so I would remember special things about people. That day I wrote the word dead across twenty-six names. A common thread ran through all those names. They were all good-hearted and gentle human beings. It was then I realized my community had been devastated, and I was living amid a modern-day holocaust. I no longer felt lucky.

Perhaps that list, with my little personal notes, might serve as a memorial to the devastation that surrounded us.

Vance Britenriker (11/1/63 artist)
Lee Brevard (Paris 79 jewelry)
Billy Bernardo (free cards)
Al Gamberg (Macy's and Atlanta design)

Jon Gould (Paramount/Warhol/Paris 15 Rue Cherche Midi)

Kenny Satcha (Sports Connection drag)

Phil Gunnison (friend of Bruce Dizon)

Keith Haring (call at home only/secretary Julia Gruen)

Ernie Cruthers (Studio 1/invites/V.I.P.)

Greg Stewart (Pepperdine w/Kevin F./brother's Bruce)

Sheldon Andleson (Bank of L.A.)

Richard Garner (CPA)

David Pollard (lawyer/call in car)

Eugene Reiman (met with Jim Brooker)

George Crowly (Stan's boyfriend)

David Sholtis (doc's friend/Atlanta T.J.'s friend)

John (from Kevin Fowler Cheesecake Factory)

Patrick McGuire (Albert's friend)

Arthur Promoff (Cliff/works for David Geffen)

Bruce Weintraub (design L.A.)

Eric Fisher (Wayne)

Bill Miller (the Athletic Club)

Dan Stone (A Course in Miracles)

Billy Jackson (friend of Billy Bologna)

Doug Harrison (J.T.)

Lance Stugart (hair)

We often lose contact with people due to life changes, but when death makes that choice for us, it is very different. I broke down weeping as I read those names — and the only conclusion I drew was that life was meaningless.

In 1990, in the Athletic Club in Los Angeles, Albert and I met again. The club had become a somewhat run-down place. It had been a popular gym years before. Now it was filled with AIDS patients trying to hold on to what was left of their bodies.

I was in the locker room, and saw an elegant man. Neither one of us recognized the other. It wasn't too surprising; many years had passed. Albert had some plastic surgery done, and I was older and no longer into bodybuilding. Both of us had traveled far. We had fast-paced lives. Thousands of names and faces had crossed our paths since Miami.

There we stood. Albert glanced at me. I glanced at him. After all those years, we now both found each other attractive. During the next few weeks, we exchanged casual smiles and courteous hellos at the gym, but still didn't recognize each other from the past. I was at the club's cafe one day, eating lunch after a workout, and Albert came up and asked if he could join me. We talked for several hours, and still didn't recognize each other from Miami. The conversation flowed effortlessly.

After a while, Albert put his hand on my thigh. He squeezed it and asked if I wanted to go home with him. On a primal level, I would have loved to have had sex with him, but I had hopes of finding a true and special love. I picked his hand off and politely declined, telling him that I thought we would become great friends.

Albert smiled and showed no visible sign of disappointment. That confirmed my suspicion that had I accepted his advance, I would have been only one of many conquests. I had watched him, during the preceding weeks at the gym, offering that same seductive smile to others, and I had decided to pursue a platonic friendship only. This friendship grew beyond anything I could have predicted. It became a relationship that would alter my entire life.

In the days and weeks that followed, our conversations rapidly deepened. We spoke about our pasts, and finally realized we had known each other years before. This was a strong and delightful revelation. The intense joy of having known each other when we were so much younger fueled our friendship. We joked and reminisced about our shared history, and talked every day.

After a while, I shared with Albert a few simple sentences that completely changed our relationship. Those words allowed Albert to trust me, and to love me. That trust would form a bond that would transcend death's wall of silence.

We were sitting in the health club's cafe and I told him something that one of my most insightful friends, Sharon Shaw, had once told me. I said, "Albert, I want you to know something about me. It's important, because you're becoming such a good friend. I like you and care about you very much. I am not a person who judges others. Please don't ever feel ashamed with me about anything you have ever done. I will never judge you. No matter what, I am always going to be your friend."

He looked at me with a glistening tear in his eye, and gently asked me if I meant what I had just said. I told him I did. Suddenly that tear became an avalanche, and he cried and cried and told me all his secrets, all his shame. He poured out emotions he had held in for years.

I took him outside, and we walked for several blocks, and then sat in the shade of an old ficus tree. He emptied his heart and bared his soul. He told me he was HIV-positive. He told me he had worked as a prostitute, and about his plastic surgery. As he talked, his body language was defensive — he sat as though he wanted to run away, or expected to be punished. But nothing in his confession distressed or shocked me. After all, I too was living with AIDS. I too had prostituted myself twice as a teenager, and I certainly had my own moments of vanity.

When he finished, I said, "Is that all? I thought there'd be something really terrible, like you killed someone."

He grinned, and he asked me straight out to never abandon him. I told him we would be friends for life. We hugged each other, and his mood lightened. Our friendship and love had found roots.

Albert had also experienced the devastation of friends lost to AIDS. He knew the importance of what we felt for each other. He needed me as much as I needed him. In a time of such great loss and despair, we quickly bonded. The connection from our childhood and Albert's trust in me solidified our relationship. It seemed remarkable to share stories that were more than a decade old with someone. At that time in my life, a decade seemed much longer than it does today. I was thrilled to have someone who had been present through the hardships of youth, and who had now returned to confront the hardships that life with AIDS had brought.

It's fascinating how a single conversation or event can sometimes spark a deep relationship. From that day on we saw each other every day. Eventually, we understood each other without words. The intertwining of our relationship became more intense and strange as our years together progressed. People would sometimes comment that it seemed as if we had become one soul in two bodies.

All of my friendships became more meaningful

to me during this period. I had four close friends at the time: Albert, Mark Simon, Tony Hamilton, and Kelly Cole. Life was not the same as it was before AIDS. I felt changes within my body, emotionally and physically. The script had changed, and so did the flavor of life. On one hand, life was harder; on the other, the texture of each day seemed to be richer. Time was more precious. To some extent, I had adjusted to the flow of the river. I was sailing along quite nicely, friends in tow. The five of us had enough energy for going out to the movies or theater. We even had time for talks of politics and fund raising. It was a joy to have these friends. We were all dealing with AIDS. We were a family.

Back then, I loved to cook, and the five of us would get together at my place once or twice a week. After dinner, we played cards. It wasn't the food or cards that brought us together, though. It was the company we enjoyed. We had become an impromptu support group. We spent more time talking than paying attention to the game. Interruptions were frequent, and sometimes we forgot all about the game, lost in conversations about our lives, art, politics, and love. Most of those nights, we laughed and joked. Somehow we were able to forget AIDS.

It was always Albert who led the conversations into spirituality. He was the most serious among us.

We figured his questions had something to do with his Catholic background. Once the subject was opened, no one hesitated to share his opinion. It was natural that we would discuss death and ponder an afterlife. Yet, spirituality was an abstract idea for all five of us. We were all skeptics to varying degrees. Albert had the most faith in the possibility of an afterlife. I didn't rule out the possibility, but certainly had no proof of it. And, considering the times, I needed proof.

One night, Albert came up with the idea of taking an oath to contact the others from beyond. His eyes glistened with excitement at the prospect. Tony seemed to approve of the idea, but Mark and Kelly merely patronized the "silly concept," and didn't take it seriously. It was too strange an idea for them. Perhaps I took it a bit more seriously only because of my love and admiration for Albert. As a group, we never again spoke of the idea.

Months after Albert's suicide, I asked the other three if they remembered the oath. Kelly and Mark didn't even remember the conversation, and Tony only vaguely remembered our promise. He smiled and made a joke about it. If I talk to Albert, he said, I should ask him for the five hundred dollars Albert had borrowed from him. Tony always had a sarcastic wit.

Tony and I had met on New Year's Eve in 1976,

and had been friends a long time. When we met, he was modeling in New York City. He received a lot of attention for his looks, and had some success in modeling before he took to acting. Our friendship was one that I never quite understood. We were opposites in many ways. Like Albert, Tony had no common sense. Perhaps that vulnerability is what sparked the friendship. Despite our differences, the chemistry was right from the first day we met.

Kelly was the son of Nat King Cole. He entered my life later, in the early eighties, when he started to date Tony. Kelly was a brilliant young person, but spoiled rotten. I disliked him immediately. He was a snob. I believed he only had use for me because of my intimate friendship with Tony. At least, that's what I assumed at first. His father had died when he was very young, and I assumed he was spoiled as a result of that.

It was not until years later that I heard the story of his childhood. Kelly had been adopted. It had been Nat's idea, according to Kelly. When Nat King Cole died, Kelly became an unwanted burden. Years later Kelly told me that his sister and mother had denied him money for a cancer treatment not covered by his insurance. That story finally made me see Kelly's pain, but I had no way of knowing that when we met. Kelly's arrogance masked great suffering.

Kelly and Tony stopped dating, and I didn't run

into Kelly again until 1986. He had changed, for the better. Being HIV-positive had humbled him, and made him softer. He dealt with it in such a good way — I wish more people could deal with suffering and loss in such a manner. He was more open and compassionate. Suffering does that to some people; other people can become bitter. I ran into Kelly in Santa Monica, and he invited me over for coffee. We reminisced, and he confessed that he was having financial problems. I agreed to loan him some money and, contrary to the old adage, it brought us much closer together. Kelly and I were better friends for the rest of his life. He completed our little family.

In the six months prior to June 1, 1994, Albert and I watched the health of Tony, Kelly, and Mark Simon decline. We feared it reflected our own path. They were sick and in the hospital more days than not. They looked more like Auschwitz survivors than the handsome, sweet, kind human beings they were a year before. Yet together, we kept our chins up and marched forward.

Mark Simon had been my first true love. We had met at a Los Angeles nightclub called Studio One. A mutual friend introduced him to me. He had no interest in me at all. I found out later he was teaching aerobics, and I attended his classes for weeks before he finally conceded to go to lunch with me. After several dates, our relationship started to evolve.

Mark's health was declining more rapidly than anyone else's in our little group. It seemed as though he had every opportunistic infection imaginable. He had zero T-cells for seven years. Not even his doctors could understand why he was still alive. I am certain it was his strong will to live and his great reservoir of denial. Mark never believed he would ever die. He seemed to think of AIDS as if it were a cold he would get over. At the end, one of the last things he struggled to say was, "I'll get over this soon. I've been in bed for almost a year. I have a lot of time to make up for. I am too young for this." It's sad that he was completely serious, and only partially correct.

Mark was the youngest of our group, and his deterioration was the hardest to watch. He had so much joy and love for life. He was filled with plans for the future until his last breath. Albert and I visited him often in the hospital. Each time, we were certain he would die. Each time, according to statistics, he should have died. To our amazement, he would somehow bounce back, but only to suffer again. We had dated and been friends since 1985. He died in 1995, after Albert and Tony, and like them died too young.

Mark was an inspiration for all of us. His ability to find hope in even the darkest moments kept him alive years beyond medical reason. But it was not long enough — if only the new drugs had been available months earlier, Mark would likely have survived AIDS.

When Tony died in 1995, Kelly and I were quite ill. Unlike Mark, Tony had given up. He had made some money from the *Mission Impossible* television series, and had other small royalties coming in. He had built his acting career on his rugged, virile good looks, however, and when his energy and appearance failed, he lost his ability to work. For Tony, his acting career was everything.

All his life, Tony had spent more money than he earned. Now he was broke. While he was hospitalized, his condominium was repossessed by the bank. He was without hope and, by early 1994, he just wanted to die. That year he got sicker and sicker until he finally did. I am convinced a stronger will to live would have saved Tony.

Before Albert died, he and I often tried to lift Tony's spirits. We tried to convince him to fight for his life. We took him out often, and lied to him and told him he looked great. But, by 1994, our efforts did little good. Tony had surrendered his will to fight against AIDS.

Toward the end of his life, he gave me a photograph of himself signed, "To a brave hero. Love, Tony." I asked him what he meant, and he said, "You know, Joel, I'm just not a hero like you. AIDS is a war like any other war — there will be casualties and heroes."

He said I was an inspiration to him because I fought on as the battles raged. I never felt like an inspiration, but I treasure that compliment.

By 1995, Kelly had dementia, and I found it difficult to spend time with him. I was fighting my own health battles and reeling from Albert's suicide. We met for coffee, just once or twice a month. He was often in his own dream world. Time with him felt strained.

I sometimes think that Kelly may have been the luckiest one of the four, that perhaps he never quite realized what was going on around him. He would often tell me he had just been with Tony, Mark, or Albert, and he'd describe in great detail their imaginary visits. Without fail, he would berate me for not joining their festivities.

One of the last times I saw Kelly, he showed up in full riding gear. He was wearing Gucci riding boots and a hat, and carrying a crop. He told me he had just played polo against Prince Charles's team. He was very sad.

"Where were you?" he said. "Our team lost. Mark and Tony were there to cheer me on. Maybe if you'd been there putting some energy into this, we would have won."

I was stunned. I had tried at other times, to no avail, to pull him back to reality. I stuttered an apology.

Kelly was the last of the group to enter my life and the last to leave. When he died in 1996, I wrote the word *dead* across four more names.

CHAPTER 3

Our Promise to Signal

Thank God I had Albert by my side as long as I did. We needed each other.

Every morning Albert would wake me with a loving phone call, and each night I would tuck him into bed by phone. Almost every day we did something together, usually lunch, dinner, a movie, or a workout. No matter what we did, we had fun. Together, we could forget about AIDS. Together, we laughed and smiled as we had as teenagers in the seventies.

It was strange — even on days when we didn't make plans, we kept running into each other, at odd times and in odd places. It became a regular occurrence — and Los Angeles is a very big city, and Albert and I lived on opposite sides of town. It happened often during Albert's final year — sometimes three times a week. I still don't understand how or why it would happen so often. I didn't ponder it when he was alive, I simply enjoyed these surprise encounters. They were a time for a fun-break.

One time when we ran into each other, we decided to pull over at the first restaurant we saw and grab a salad. Two younger gay men were in the restaurant, both obviously very ill. One was covered with Kaposi's sarcoma cancer lesions and the other could hardly walk. Both of them weighed under a hundred pounds. I was more affected than Albert seemed to be. My mood dropped, and I asked if that was our future. For the first time, I saw a rare moment of strength in Albert. He turned to me and said defiantly, "That's their path, not ours." I felt reassured. My mood and the conversation shifted.

That line became our creed. Whenever doubt or fear arose in one of us about surviving AIDS, the other would say, "That is not our path." This simple phrase became a tremendous source of strength. We were able to reinforce each other with this belief.

Then I got a viral inner ear infection. It was quite painful and I avoided pain medication because I wanted to take only medication that battled the disease, not the symptoms. My dear friend Sharon suggested I try biofeedback or self-hypnosis. I doubted their effectiveness, but I was desperate, and consulted a well-known hypnotherapist, Melvin Cohen, M.D. Some important things came out of the one session I had with him. His wisdom was more valuable than the hypnosis itself.

First, I learned a lesson in forgiveness. I came to a new level of understanding what forgiveness means. I had always felt forgiveness was the ability to look beyond the immediate anger or hurt and find the reasons behind the other's actions, and then let go. Dr. Cohen put another spin on it. He said that forgiveness is a conscious act that we do for ourselves, not for anyone else. When we are wronged or hurt, we have only two choices: we can either stay with the bad feelings, and keep them inside where they will fester and cause disease, or we can make the conscious choice to let go of them for our own sake. Letting go releases the anger and hurt, to our own benefit.

The second thing I learned from Dr. Cohen was about the nature of disease. He convinced me that no disease in the history of humankind has been 100 percent fatal. Some diseases can be 99 percent fatal, but none are 100 percent. The small percentage of people who survived those diseases did so on their own mental and inner strength, on their will to live, and through a concentrated effort to eliminate all negative thoughts.

The hypnosis session became a conscious effort to eliminate self-sabotage. I slowed down into a relaxed state, and I became aware of my own negative self-talk. All of us have this to one degree or another. I began carefully taking note of the negative messages I sent to myself. Slowly, over time, I began letting go of them. I saw them as an enemy that I could not afford to keep.

Armed with these two pieces of insight, I became determined to survive AIDS. I wanted to be in that small percentage of survivors, no matter what. I tried to share what I learned in the hypnosis session with Albert.

A new aspect of our friendship began to emerge. Together we searched for meaning in our lives, and questions about the hereafter began to surface. We both started to do volunteer work at AIDS hospices. Somehow, supporting others took us out of our own distress. This time in our lives was important to both of us. We explored our ideas, fears, and hopes about dying. We read many books, including *Many Lives, Many Masters* by Brian Weiss, M.D., *Life After Life* by Raymond Moody, M.D., *Man's Search for Meaning* by Viktor Frankl, M.D., and *The Tibetan Book of the Dead.*

We found certain similarities in some of these readings, similarities that defined a truth we felt in our core, a truth we believed as children: There is life after these lives end, and we are all connected, in some mysterious form.

Spirituality was still an abstract concept for both

of us, but during this time we became hopeful skeptics. We hoped for the possibility of life after death. We hoped certain souls were destined to meet again. Neither of us, however, felt that our past lives, if they existed, were pertinent to this life, or that it was important that we know about them. We speculated that if there were such a thing as reincarnation, we had been together before. Ours was too deep and strong a relationship to be understood within the confines of one lifetime. Our paths constantly collided, as if destiny kept pushing us together. A lot of time would pass before this made sense to me.

When the group made the promise to contact each other after death, it was almost in jest. But Albert and I talked about it several times after that, and we agreed we would try. We swore we would try to signal one another as an assurance of life after death. We both wanted to believe there was something beyond this world and its suffering.

Albert was very enthusiastic about this oath. His belief in an afterlife was stronger than mine. He brought the subject up many times, and read more about it than I did. He continued this exploration long after I had tired of it. Even though the others had forgotten the commitment, Albert and I were intent on keeping it.

I had formed a simple spiritual view. It's best

described with the following story:

We watched a television debate one Sunday between a famous rabbi and a cardinal on the subject of the differences between Christianity and Judaism. The rabbi concluded his assertions by saying, "It's quite simple. For two thousand years, Christians have believed that mankind is intrinsically bad, that all human beings inherit original sin and always must go to God for forgiveness. Jews, on the other hand, for four thousand years, have tended to believe mankind is intrinsically good. We do make mistakes, however, and should go to God for forgiveness when we do so."

Albert and I talked about this, and decided both religions have God as an outside source — a huge omnipotent and detached figure — whereas we had come to believe that God was inside all of us. God is present everywhere, so we are all collectively part of God. It is as if we are all infinitesimally tiny grains of sand on a giant beach, and the beach is God. And we each have a responsibility to polish our own grain of sand so the beach is as radiant as possible.

For many months, Albert and I continued to have talks about life after death. It was always late at night, and Albert always initiated the conversation.

As we approached 1994, my health failed, and I neared my lowest point. I feared I would soon die. I planned for my death in all the normal ways. I made a will, with a medical power of attorney, and I made burial plans. Our pact was bonded through the suffering around us.

I meant to keep my promise. If there was any way possible I would signal Albert. I loved him in so many ways. I hoped God might allow me to flicker some lights, or *something*. It might seem like a parlor game or séance spectacle to some people, but I knew it would be real to Albert. He had become a bit like a younger brother to me. It was my deepest hope that if I passed on, I would still be able to shine a bit of hope for him.

CHAPTER 4

The First Contact

June 2, 1994

Albert's suicide triggered an avalanche of painful memories. Every loss I had ever experienced in life rose to the surface. I thought seriously of suicide; a large part of me did not want to live. It seemed the perfect solution. I might even see Albert again. I too had the drugs at home. We had gotten them together in Mexico. What was the point of continuing my struggle? The prognosis for those with AIDS was grim. Tony, Kelly, and Mark would soon be dead. I felt weak, and the person I looked to for strength was gone. All I could feel was pain and anger. I couldn't believe the bastard had done it.

I had lost other friends, but this was different. My best friend was gone, by his own hands, unexpectedly. I still had so many unanswered questions.

A cloud formed that day in June. It would be months before it began to lift. That evening, I had no way of knowing it would ever lift. I was without hope.

I left Albert's home, tightly clutching his note in my hands. A friend drove me home. That place had always been a nest for me. It was filled with treasured collectibles, pictures, and memories. I paced the apartment for what seemed like hours. For the first time, I was lost among those memories. At the time I needed Albert the most, he had abandoned me. He was the one person I could call for help and comfort. Now, as much as I needed my best friend, he was gone. I cried and paced. I had not eaten all day. Finally exhaustion took over and I lay down on my bed.

I took a deep breath, then several more. I was restless and couldn't sleep. I stared at the ceiling, cold and alone.

About one in the morning, I felt a chill. It was a hot California night and suddenly I was very cold. I sensed Albert was near and, for some reason, this made me panic. I reached across my bed and grabbed the phone and called Sharon. I woke her from a deep sleep. I was shaking.

I said, "Sharon, I think Albert is coming to visit me." She knew I was frightened.

"You have nothing to fear," she said. "Albert loved you, and would never hurt you."

Her words were exactly what I needed to hear. Those few simple words comforted me. I was instantly calm. I thanked her and said good night and put the receiver in its cradle.

In less than a second, I felt a warm flush of heat, and I could feel Albert's presence again. I couldn't move a muscle, not even blink. I was calm and relaxed. I felt no physical or emotional pain while he was present. For the next few moments, all of my sadness evaporated.

There is a distinct line between conscious and unconscious thought. I was definitely conscious, clearly awake. I was not in the dreamlike state one experiences before falling asleep. Like the character played by Jodie Foster in the movie *Contact,* I have no evidence other than my own story. I never really expected Albert to contact me. Before his death, spirituality remained an abstract idea, but at 2 A.M. on the morning of June 2, 1994, I was given a concrete spiritual experience.

A transparent light appeared above my bed. It was a thin light, veiled in some way. It looked like smoke rising above candlelight. My room was very dark. My blackout shades were pulled shut. There were no lights on. The misty light hovered above me and, again, I could sense Albert's words in some way, not by hearing them, but by feeling them clearly. They were strong and distinct. He began with a question.

You know it's me, don't you?

I couldn't answer, I was incapable of moving. Yet

I felt as comfortable as a sleeping baby. I felt coddled. All pain was gone. I was with Albert again. After a moment, I was able to raise a hand and wave at the light to answer yes. It was a wave I had used as a very young child, folding my fingers to the palm of my hand.

Good, this is for you, not for me. You need what I am about to give you. It is the most I can give you. You cannot handle more. You would implode if you knew what I now know.

His thoughts and words, his message, streamed down over me. Each word felt different. This communication was vastly different from anything I had ever experienced or even imagined. It is difficult to describe with words what it felt like. I stared in amazement at the light. I could see through it. It was more like a fog than a light. I listened, fascinated, unable to move. Albert continued.

You need what I am about to give you. It's less than a pinpoint of what I now know. It's a tiny molecule, less than a speck of dust from where I am. But it will carry you through the rest of your life. You will understand, because of our love, trust, and knowledge of each other. I must be brief, I don't have a lot of time.

I remained immobile, transfixed by the luminescence above my bed. I sensed Albert was not alone, that others were with him, guiding him, and that he had somehow been given this time between worlds. His communication became stronger and even more intense.

I felt safe and relaxed. The faint light was real. It was different from anything I had ever known, or ever seen, or could have imagined. It was a gift that I am now honored to share.

You will understand more through my suicide. When I was alive, I thought life was only worthwhile if things were going good. If I had my health, money, or a good love life, then it had meaning. Life was worth living when it was going the way I thought it should. I now know differently.

Joel, you must not take your own life. You must go as far as you can in life. Know that each and every moment of life matters and that they are the same in many ways. Ways you have not yet seen. The good, the bad, the healthy days, the sick ones, happy, sad, bored, or thrilled — they are the same. With each and every breath, and in every moment of life, you are working things out, things that are connected to something far greater. You are a part of something much bigger. We are all a part of this larger purpose. Those kind people and those cruel people all have a purpose you can't possibly understand right now. Each and every person matters, and each and every moment matters. The painful ones included. We are all one.

You are now confined to living a single moment at a time. Moment by moment, you mark your life. All spiritual growth is based on work from the past. All past experiences are building blocks. All the individual moments of life are the grains of matter that form each block. We are more than grains of sand on a collective beach that is God — we are individual universes bound, tied, and connected to one another.

Individual spiritual growth is connected to a collective growth. Free will and destiny are two paths that head to the same place. They cross each other along the way. They are inseparable. Nor is the individual separate from the whole. All life forces are evolving, growing, and moving forward toward oneness with the infinite.

You must live as many of life's moments as you can endure. There is meaning and purpose in every breath of life for you — and for everyone — including the moments of pain and suffering. All suffering is connected to a greater good you can't possibly understand right now.

Each breath, each second of life matters. In every breath and moment of life, you are indeed accomplishing and working out so much that you can't understand or recognize from where you are now.

Trust me, trust in our love. You will learn and grow through my death. You will know it was my path and destiny to end my life in that moment. It was my life's lesson. What I've now given you is a tiny molecule of the lessons I've learned since death. My suicide is also connected to a greater good. You will see it, in part, unfold in your own life. I will contact you again. I am with you always.

A wave of intense feelings swelled up, exactly what I felt earlier, anger and pain. I started to scream. "You bastard, you left me!" I could move again, and gestured wildly. I yelled, "Get out of here, leave!"

The light and Albert vanished. Perhaps he was gone before I even spoke. I was cold and empty again.

I woke Sharon again from her deep sleep. I was confused, and mumbled to her what had just happened. I could not convey the enormity of it all. Instinctively, I believed no one would ever understand. I said good-bye, and stayed up all night.

Albert's words echoed in my mind for hours. My epiphany had begun, and his words stuck in my mind like a haunting melody. I did not understand the bulk of his message, and it would take years to fully digest, but his words immediately gave me a tiny bit of hope during that dark time.

I remained emotionally wrecked for several months. I was at my lowest point that night, but his message made some sense to me. Albert had contacted me.

That first encounter was multi-leveled, with many messages within it. It planted a seed of hope that prevented my suicide, and will carry me through the rest of my life. Because I experienced it firsthand, there was little room for skepticism, but I somehow managed to maintain most of mine. Even after that night, I still held on to most of my doubts, and I wanted further proof.

Despite this, his message created a sense of resolve deep within me. His message — that all the moments of life matter, that each and every second we are working things out, that suffering is connected to a greater good — rang true to my core. I began to make choices based on those words. They kept me fighting for my life. My sense of resolve deepened. After sad or painful events, even sometimes during them, I began to find a certain sense of peace. Perhaps peace is not the right word for what I feel. *Acceptance* may be closer to it.

I believe that every moment of life is indeed precious. I have further learned to believe events that appear horrible must serve a purpose, a purpose I cannot possibly understand. If any good could come from my suffering or from his suicide, then good might come from any suffering.

Now I fully believe Albert's words. On some deep level, I know the truth of two old sayings: "You are in the right place at the right time, or you would be somewhere else," and "Don't fight the river, it flows on its own." This sense of acceptance was new to me in 1994. It took years to solidify within me. It doesn't take pain away, but it has affected the outcome of many decisions. The lessons I have learned since that night answered many questions about injustices and suffering. Part of the answer was simply not to question that which has no answer. The other part became a clear, solid belief that all of life is connected to something larger. Perhaps we cannot see this in our lifetime. As Albert said:

We all are working things out that most of us never realize while we are alive.

CHAPTER 5

A Tiny Signal, Albert's Memorial

June 5, 1994

Four days after Albert's death, Steve wanted to hold a memorial in Albert's garden. Steve was an ex-boyfriend of Albert's. After their relationship ended, they had stayed together as roommates. Their relationship, however, was tumultuous. Steve was a socialite and could not miss an opportunity for a party. At that time, memorials were a common event in the gay community. They had become less sad, less serious than one might expect. Steve asked me to speak at the memorial. I still felt devastated, but I accepted.

I arrived about 3:20 P.M. It all seemed very strange. Only a few old friends of Albert's were present. For the most part, it was a gathering of Steve's friends. I knew only a fraction of the people. I had expected Albert's friends would get together and reflect on the gentle soul we had just lost. The drinks were flowing, and I felt like an outsider. I sat down in the garden and my mind wandered to the countless hours Albert and I had spent planting that beautiful garden.

An odd thought struck me: we had placed hummingbird feeders in the garden some time ago, but had never once seen a hummingbird there. I speculated that the thirty or more cats that lived in Albert's backyard had scared the birds away. Albert used to trap stray cats in the neighborhood and take them in to be spayed. He said that kittens of alley cats have little chance of surviving, and it was his way of preventing their tragic little deaths. Although he released the cats after they had been spayed, he felt obligated to continue feeding them. He put out milk and food every night, and most of the cats in the neighborhood took advantage of the free buffet. I guessed the cats scared all the birds away, but I was never quite sure. All I knew was that the garden was without hummers.

As I sat in the garden, one of Albert's more unusual friends sat down next to me. His name was Ed Foley. Years before, he and Albert had worked together. In recent years, they had become friends. It was something I never understood. Ed possessed most of the traits I disliked in people. He was a conservative Republican and an ex–police officer. He was gruff, and he drank heavily and constantly smoked the stinkiest pipe I have ever smelled. We had absolutely nothing in common. Yet there we were, sharing thoughts about the friend we had just lost.

I mentioned my disappointment in the party-like atmosphere. I said perhaps I wouldn't eulogize Albert. I wondered why more people weren't sad. I wanted the whole world to be in mourning.

Ed said, "Forget the strangers and remember Albert."

We talked for an hour or more, and then Steve asked me to speak to the crowd. I stood with Ed to my right and Steve to my left. Suddenly, a tiny ruby-throated hummingbird fluttered and hovered above me. I pointed the bird out to Ed, who said, "Forget the bird and say something." I wondered for a moment — was the bird a signal? Then I began my unrehearsed eulogy.

I told the crowd that it was difficult to explain Albert's suicide, even though I knew him so well. I understood his suffering. Albert was someone who was never satisfied. If he held the moon in his hands, he would struggle to reach the stars. As he had said many times, he was his own worst enemy. He always looked at himself with far too critical an eye. He was extremely sensitive and gentle. The brutality of nature was difficult for him to face on a daily basis. Life was more than he could handle.

Albert had once said he felt as if he were a stranger on this planet. I understood this now. I felt like a stranger. He questioned how people could be so cruel; he could not understand his fellow man. He thought the world was a brutal place. All around him friends were sick, and suffering seemed to be everywhere.

I stood before Albert's friends and went on to describe the virtues of the timid and kind person I knew and loved. I paused for a moment, and remembered some of Albert's words from the night he came to me. I told the crowd that I felt he had come to visit me the night he died, that his words had comforted me, and that his suicide was perhaps his destiny, his life's lesson. I said I was certain that Albert was now exactly where he wanted to be, that he was in a better place, and that I was hopeful he was watching over those he loved. I wanted to explain what I experienced the night Albert came, but it wasn't easy. I didn't think anyone would believe me. I tried, though, hoping maybe I could plant the tiny seed of hope I had been given. Albert's words were etched on my soul, and even though I felt lost, I was able to touch upon some of his message.

When I looked out over the crowd of friends that had gathered, I realized many of his dear friends were crying. I closed the short eulogy with Albert's favorite quotation, an ancient Chinese saying:

"Meeting is the beginning of parting."

When I finished speaking, I was ready to go home. Ed lived near me, and asked for a ride. Night had settled in and I welcomed the company.

As we drove, I felt Albert's presence again. It felt as if he was asking me to be friends with Ed, telling me that Ed was completely alone in this world and needed my friendship. I felt a strange obligation to befriend him.

We talked as we drove across town, and I felt a bit of warmth towards Ed. When we arrived at his apartment building, we sat outside in my car and reminisced for about an hour about the friend we'd lost.

When Ed got out to leave, I felt an urge to hug him. I got out of the car, and we held each other in the moonlight for about five minutes, both crying. My eyes wandered up to a telephone line above us, and there sat another ruby-throated hummingbird, making its throaty little chirping sound. Ed wasn't too impressed when I pointed it out.

"So what? A hummingbird." But I wondered again, was it a signal?

A year later I discovered hummingbirds don't come out at night. They go into a state of hibernation called *torpor,* in which their heart rate and breathing slows down to conserve energy. They become vulnerable at night, and consequently, sleep through it.

When I reminded Ed of that night and the tiny bird, and showed him my book on the behavior of hummingbirds, the uniqueness of the situation seemed to register. He was beginning to look at Albert's passing from a more spiritual viewpoint. He said he hoped Albert was in heaven, looking down over us.

The next day, I received a letter from Albert in the mail. It was a cleaned-up version of the crumpled note, on stationery engraved with forget-me-not flowers.

It was Albert's final acknowledgment that he really loved me. The note ended with, "Please, don't ever forget me."

I skimmed the note when it arrived, but was in too much pain to understand its significance.

CHAPTER 6

The Following Months

June–October 1994

I never expected the intensity or volume of signals that followed. Perhaps I was less able to receive his signals early on because of my health. I faced months of illness after Albert's memorial. I felt my body aging more rapidly. My energy level dropped. There were more bouts with infections, and I was constantly nauseous. Simple errands took more energy than I possessed. I lay motionless in bed for hours, drained. Hours in bed became days in bed — then weeks, then months. My shades were drawn, and I lost track of time. I seldom knew what day of the week it was. This may explain the time gap between Albert's first signals and those that followed.

When I forced myself to leave the house, I had no balance. I went to the grocery store and struggled not to fall down. The few times I did venture out, I ran into old acquaintances, and they were horrified, and didn't know what to say. I had lost a lot of weight;

death must have been written across my face.

Something inside, a tiny spark of hope, kept me going. It may have been Albert's message. I didn't worry about the time I had lost. I was grateful to be in a safe and comfortable space. Even moments of moderate pain, after periods of great pain, boosted my faith that I would regain my health. I was reaching for a middle ground, a place where I might not be getting better, but wouldn't be getting any worse. It felt like an intense flu, and I focused on moments of less pain. If my breathing was labored, I chose to focus on how good it felt when it hadn't been.

There were times, though, when I wanted to die. Many others had died with less serious infections. From the viewpoint of the medical establishment, I didn't have a chance. I had every excuse in the world to take my own life, but deep within my core, that little spark of hope kept me alive. It strengthened my will to live.

Sharon Shaw called me daily and visited often. She continuously reinforced the idea that the illness would pass, and she forced me to focus on any good there had been, even if it had been brief. She helped me survive the bad days by focusing on good moments and better days. An open window with a pleasant breeze meant so much — the sunshine, the trees outside. Each hour without pain revitalized my spirit.

Eventually, I had a few good days. Many of my physiological problems began responding to treatment.

After about five months, I started getting out of the house more often. I began with a walk around the block a few times a week. Ultimately, I was able to run small errands. When I slipped backward, Sharon reminded me of each good day. I drew strength from her conviction and, slowly, I was healing.

Six months after Albert's death, the grief began to soften. I started a new series of treatments, and my physical condition continued to improve. Gradually, I regained my strength. I returned to the gym. Five minutes on the Stairmaster was grueling, but as time passed, I was able to spend thirty minutes. I felt more and more alive, and my recovery accelerated. I attribute much of this improvement to protease inhibitors, a newly available treatment. My blood counts got closer and closer to normal. I felt I'd been given a new lease on life, and I hoped Albert was with me. I thought of him often, and when I didn't, something unusual — some "coincidence" — would remind me of him.

One day as I left the gym, for instance, Bette Midler's song, "Wind Beneath My Wings," was playing over the sound system. I've got nothing against Bette Midler, but I've never cared much for love ballads or pop music.

When I got to my car, I'd left my radio on, tuned to 103.5 "Coast Radio," where callers were invited to dedicate songs to someone they loved. As I turned on the engine, I heard the announcer say, "Here it is, because he loves you —" and again, "Wind Beneath My Wings" began to play. Enough of that, I thought, as I reached for a cassette tape from a bunch I kept in the car. It was dark; I grabbed the first one I could reach and put it in the deck and, again, to my amazement, "Wind Beneath My Wings" came soaring out of the speakers. I pulled over to the side of the road and looked at the tape, and remembered I had put some of Albert's old compilation tapes in my car a few days before. This was one of them, cued right up to the same song.

It seemed the universe was trying to force it on me, and I felt compelled to sit there and actually listen to it. I found it very touching. The lyrics spoke of deep love and friendship, and I couldn't help but wonder if, somehow, Albert had arranged this coincidence. For the first time since the night he died, I felt his presence as a warm glow. Was this a hug from beyond? That's what it felt like.

It felt like he was with me at that moment. I looked up and noticed that, by coincidence, I had pulled the car over next to the huge old ficus tree we had sat under years before, the day Albert poured his soul out to me, and expressed his shame.

I drove home filled with the warm glow. I felt refreshed and comforted. The lyrics reminded me of every positive thing Albert had ever said to me. A reminder from beyond? I was still skeptical, yet it really didn't matter whether it was coincidence or not — I had more optimism, and *that* was saving my life.

A few days later, I decided to go to a church and pray. When I look back on it, I think I was hoping for a larger, more definite signal. I thought if there was anywhere Albert would be able to reach me, it would be there. Albert had taken me to the place in 1993. It wasn't a church really, it was a chapel in a convent of cloistered nuns, who sell their own baked bread. It's unlike anywhere else in Los Angeles, a tiny oasis of calm, right in the middle of Hollywood, off Vine.

The minute I went into the chapel, I was over-whelmed with emotion and began to cry. I was flooded with memories. I thought of all the pain Albert had endured during his life. I was aware how deeply he must have been hurting to take his own life.

After an hour of prayer, I headed towards my car, and an elderly nun approached me. She was the only nun at the convent who was able to speak; the others had taken vows of silence. She asked why I was cry-ing, and I told her my best friend had taken his own life. She remembered Albert often coming in alone to pray.

"He must have suffered a lot," she said. I said he had. "We all suffer in this life," she said softly.

For years, I have thought about that moment, and about those six words. We do all suffer in this life. I hadn't received the signal I was looking for, but her words stayed with me, and I began to wonder if suffering were a part of some universal cleansing process. In time, I began to believe it was. If we are all a cell in the body of God, all connected in this universe, perhaps our suffering functions the way the liver functions in the body; perhaps suffering cleanses the greater being.

I also came to realize that we do not suffer equally. In the past, I believed all people suffered equally. I thought that what each of us experiences as pain is all the suffering we know, and to each of us, this suffering is great. I assumed one could not compare his suffering to another's, and that somehow it was all balanced — equal suffering all around. I believed that those who seemed to endure less suffering felt it more intensely, and that the more one suffered, the more he or she could tolerate. I no longer believe that to be universally true.

Some people suffer more than others. In my case, I had suffered more than the average person, and I was becoming stronger from that suffering.

I hope I can transfer this conviction to others who suffer — I am certain that there is meaning and purpose in suffering. If I am able to shine a light on someone's hope or faith in times of pain, that is probably far more significant than the documentation of any psychic events.

Circumstance, coincidence, or signals from beyond continued to remind me of Albert. One incident in particular took place in October of 1994, when I was feeling quite a bit stronger. I went to a thrift store called Out of the Closet. It felt good to be out of the house. I have always enjoyed going to thrift stores. I love rummaging through the fragmentary remains and dispossessed objects of other people's lives in hopes of finding an object I can treasure. Used objects have always held more charm for me than new ones. As I was rummaging, the staff unloaded and brought in three huge cartons of books. I glanced through them but they were uninteresting. The salesperson mentioned he had just put a box of books in the trash bin out back because they were too damaged to sell. He said I was welcome to retrieve them if I wanted.

Normally I would have declined, but I was intrigued enough to go out back and take a quick look. Most of the books were from the late nineteenth century. They were dilapidated and had acid burn, and were falling apart. I searched a little further and pulled out a book from 1878 entitled *The Meaning of Friendship*. It was in bad condition, its leather cover torn off and its binding damaged. It was a collection of quotations on friendship compiled by a priest. I took the book home and put it in an empty shoe box.

A few evenings later, I was restless and looked around for something to read. I took the little book out of the box and skimmed the text. Many of the quotations were delightful, but the pages were so fragile that several of them crumbled when I turned them. Dust fell everywhere.

When I reached the middle of the book, I found a decaying old bookmark stuck to the page. It marked a quotation underlined decades, perhaps even a century, before. The bookmark had rotted into the page where it had been placed by the last person to read it. The highlighted quotation read: *Meeting is the beginning of parting.*

My doubts that Albert had fulfilled his promise to contact me should he die first faded with moments like that. It's true that the signals over the first six months, other than the intense experience the night he died, were subtle. They could easily be considered coincidences. But for me, these quiet little signals, one after the other, offered comfort and hope. I didn't know what signals from Albert might be ahead. Perhaps to be able to receive his future gifts I needed to further heal from the suffering of that year, to clear my mind in some way. Perhaps I wasn't yet prepared to take in the profound communication that would follow.

CHAPTER 7

Hope and Signals

In November of 1994, a real estate agent and neighbor of mine persuaded me to take a look at an apartment that was just across the street. She convinced me that a move to a new building might serve as a catalyst for positive change. I wasn't entirely certain that I wanted to make such a move. I had lived in my apartment for over ten years. It was a place of comfort and safety, filled with fond memories. I was reluctant to abandon such a haven. The new apartment, though, was bigger and seemed warmer than the old. I visited the space a few times, but couldn't decide whether or not to move.

Finally, while inspecting the apartment one afternoon, I decided it would be a good move for me. The decision was quickly validated by a small, unexpected visitor. As I sat on the terrace balcony, a little hummingbird fluttered about me. The apartment was on the tenth floor of a condominium in a very urbanized section of Los Angeles. The side of the building was solid concrete — very little greenery or flowers, the attractant for hummingbirds, grew on the building's terraces. It was an austere place for that little bird; there was no reason for it to be there. My faith was growing, and I took it as a sign.

When I moved into the apartment, a hummingbird appeared at my window to greet me every morning for the first two weeks. Its twisted beak and certain markings made it identifiable as the same bird. I planted vines that encompassed the terrace and installed a red hummingbird feeder for my little visitor. Within a few weeks, the feeder had enticed more birds than I could count, feeding all day, every day. I enjoyed watching them. Their activity at the feeder was like a carefully orchestrated dance as one bird replaced another to enjoy the nectar.

The move seemed to facilitate my healing. I grew stronger with the change and felt more comfortable in the new space.

When my birthday rolled around in December, however, I felt lonely. Tony had died. Kelly and Mark were very ill and in the hospital, or they would have been with me.

I thought of the past holiday seasons when Tony, Albert, Mark, Kelly, and I had been together. The season had become something very special for all of us, a time to celebrate life and friendship. Without them, December looked bleak.

Before I met Sharon, a birthday meant very little to me. It was just another day in the year. But Sharon convinced me, with her own special enthusiasm for birthdays, that they were worthy of celebration, and they came to mean a great deal to me. She felt that commemorating a birthday, the special day each of us comes into this life, was not just festivity for the passing of another year, but a celebration of one's entire life. And each unique life was something worth ritualizing. Sharon was determined that we would celebrate my birthday.

Most of the people I have known celebrate birthdays in one of two ways. Members of one group tend to hibernate, and tell no one it's their birthday. They avoid celebrations. They go to work and behave as if it's just another day. Perhaps acknowledging the passing of time raises painful issues. The concrete marking of time can create an image of an hourglass running out of sand, a sense of time escaping from their lives, a reminder of dreams unfulfilled. If one has little faith in life after death, a birthday can be disturbing.

I think this type of person often sees the glass half empty rather than half full. "One year older, one year closer to death." This thought tugs at the bit of denial all human beings have regarding their own mortality.

I had lost this denial, and I just wanted to be with friends on my birthday. I wasn't sad, just lonely.

Another group of people tend to party on their birthdays. They remind everyone well in advance. They plan events and shout it out to the world. They see the glass half full, or perhaps they're just rejoicing in the day. Either way, they make the most of it.

By 1994, I was in this group, but I had no one except Sharon to call. I believed birthdays were a time to be surrounded by friends, a time to rejoice together and to honor our special friendships. The day the soul enters the world as we know it is indeed special. The way we celebrate our birthdays is a reflection of who we are and where we are in our lives. And the way we treat others on their birthdays is a reflection of who we are as well.

When Sharon asked what I wanted to do on my birthday, I wasn't feeling particularly well and had very little energy. I suggested a quiet dinner at a little macrobiotic restaurant on LaBrea Avenue that I'd been wanting to try.

It felt good to leave my apartment for a brief period, yet during dinner, I couldn't help feeling lonesome. We sat by a front window and talked.

Midway through dinner, a familiar face passed by the window. Our eyes met and we smiled. It was Cliff Watts, a man I dated briefly when I first moved to Los Angeles. He was an extremely kind man, a gentle and warm soul. We hadn't had much contact because he was very busy with his career. We had run into each other a few times, and spoke infrequently, once or twice a year. It was always pleasant, even special; I had secretly carried a torch for Cliff for many years. I always respected and admired him.

He tapped on the glass. With an uncharacteristically extroverted hand signal, I asked him to come inside. He asked if the food was good, and if he could join us for dinner, and I welcomed his company. We spent the next several hours talking, and it was not unlike the time Albert and I had first spoken in the cafe at the Athletic Club. I knew instantly ours would become a deeper and more meaningful friendship. Timing, the universe, or coincidence had given me a birthday present. I had a new friend.

Cliff's companionship added to my hope. He and I spent much time together throughout the next year, talking about our lives. He was fascinated by the changes that had occurred in my life. Even though he was HIV-negative, he was intrigued by my exceptionally long survival. AIDS had taught me many lessons, and he was a sponge, eager to soak them up. He learned from everyone around him, and continued to evolve. He said I had learned lessons at thirty-seven years old that many people never master in an entire lifetime. One was the ability to release things into the universe and not labor over insignificant issues. I had learned not to sweat the small stuff, and tried to live constructively in the moment. Worry seemed to be a senseless burden, and so was spending too much time thinking about the past. Mark once said, "It's okay to look at your past and learn from it, but don't stare too long. At some point, wink and go on."

I had given up making long-range plans. I didn't want to invest a lot of energy in projects or dreams that I might not live to see fulfilled. A gradual change had taken place in me, and Cliff was able to make me more aware of it. I had learned to focus on the day at hand. The expression "living on borrowed time" certainly seemed to apply to me, and affected the way I lived. In reality, we all live on borrowed time, and time is all we have. I realized that time is the essence of our lives, and human beings have an immeasurable reservoir of denial. AIDS, and a decade of death, chipped away any denial I might have clung to, and left a more grateful person in its place. I faced 1995 with hope.

As our friendship developed, I found I had someone to lean on during particularly trying days. Cliff saw me as a very strong person, and gave me positive reinforcement every day. He said, "You'll survive this. I know you will, Joel. Just think about how much you've already been through." I drew enormous strength, comfort, and courage from these soothing words.

Mark and Kelly died early in the year, and more opportunistic infections plagued me. I was blessed to have a friend supporting me. We all need to lean on those around us at certain times. Sharing an open and honest impression of how we see each other can be a great gift. A writer — I think it was Voltaire — once said, "The mirror is a worthless invention; the only way to truly see yourself is in the reflection of someone else's eyes." That is what I had always received from friends, and I'll always be grateful for it.

Despite the deaths of Tony, Kelly, and Mark, 1995 became increasingly positive for me. After many years of living with AIDS, my failing blood counts rose to near normal levels. And Albert would fulfill his promise to contact me many times during the first six months of the year. I would ponder these puzzling events for years before I decided to chronicle them in a journal.

A single event in January convinced me that Albert was not only in contact, but actually watching over me.

It was a Saturday night, and three of my new neighbors persuaded me to venture out to a party. I didn't really want to go, but went along anyway, despite my trepidation. I thought getting out would be good for me. Because I don't drink, I became the designated driver.

I was heading west on Santa Monica Boulevard approaching La Cienega, when I sensed Albert saying, *Stop the car!* It was very clear. The light in the intersection ahead was green, but I hit the brakes and came to a full stop. My passengers were startled, even irritated. Three cars passed us and went into the intersection, and a massive truck ran the red light and sped through from the other direction. The accident happened right in front of us, and involved four cars and the truck. One person was killed at the scene. It all happened so fast my passengers were in shock. One quickly apologized for being impatient. He praised my good driving.

They assumed I had seen the truck coming. I hadn't. Albert's words had been loud and distinctive in my head, and they had saved us from possible injury, or worse. I gave thanks in my prayers that night. I would never be quite the same after that. I felt more comfortable with Albert's presence, even safe, and I felt appreciative of his messages. I was more convinced than ever that they were significant. I thought it might serve me to listen carefully to them in the future.

Over time, it was becoming easier to believe that

there really was life after death. My deep skepticism was fading, and I had formed a new hypothesis: We will "see" some of the people we truly love after death.

In the book *Many Lives, Many Masters,* Dr. Brian Weiss suggests that a group of souls reincarnate together. Certain people we are close to will choose, on some "higher" level, to experience life with us again in the next life. Our relationships change, but we see each other again. I was beginning to believe that after we die, the first light we see is the soul of a loved one. That single flash of light guides us to a brighter one. The brighter one is the collective of a great number of souls.

My health improved every month. With the discovery of protease inhibitors, death had loosened its grasp on me and, in its wake, had left other gifts I would soon discover. My relationships with new friends grew, and my relationships with old friends deepened. I was not lonely. I even had an emerging social life. Many people commented on how healthy I looked. Others said I had a clarity about me they hadn't seen before. All of this was unexpected. My doctors had predicted my death in 1990. I had predicted my own death in 1994. Both these years had come and gone. Life was indeed changing.

I became convinced that other people also had

loved ones no longer alive who watched over them. It seemed logical. It would be vain of me to think this experience was unique to me.

In the years before my illness, I had made it an intention to do at least one good deed every day. I tried to do as many as I could. As I grew weaker with the illness, I became less extroverted and had less time for others. My energy was spent on healing. Now that I was feeling better, I had more time available, and became more active and outgoing. I was beginning to enjoy life once again, and there was an easier flow to life than ever before. I found myself doing favors for others again, and my life was again enriched by acts of kindness.

One day, as I was doing my good deed for the day, Albert contacted me again. It was a cool, wintry day and, while I was driving home, I saw an elderly woman struggling with a heavily loaded cart. She was attempting to push it up a hill and onto a ramp that led into an apartment complex. It looked as though the cart weighed much more than the woman, and she was quite frail. She struggled to take a step forward, then stumbled back again. I had to help her.

I pulled the car over to the side of the road and got out and asked her if I could help. She was completely delighted, and soon after, I was unloading groceries in Alice's kitchen. I had to suggest that she be more careful about who she let into her apartment in the future. She didn't seem the least bit concerned. It was refreshing.

She offered me some black currant tea — one of my favorites — and we sat and drank tea and talked for almost two hours. I studied Alice's face as she spoke. I wondered how old she was. There were many lines in her face — I guessed she was in her late eighties.

As we sat, I sensed another soul watching over her, and then I felt Albert's presence very deeply. At certain times the sensation is stronger than at other times. This time, I felt him intensely. But this was different; I clearly sensed an additional soul.

I tuned in to Albert's message: he was telling me that this woman had an older brother who had died. As old as Alice was, it would be likely that any sibling of hers would be deceased, but I also knew from this message that her brother was the soul watching over her. I asked her if she had an older brother. She told me about him and, as she spoke, the love they shared became obvious. She smiled. Her face became smoother as she spoke.

When she finished the story of her brother, she asked why I'd asked about him. I told her I had a sense that he was waiting for her and would be her "first light" when she died. She had little faith in life after death. Her face began to wrinkle again. She liked the idea, she said, but she was skeptical.

Before I left, I told her that I was sure she would see her brother again. I sensed we had both gained something from our interaction. I felt a bit more strongly that others had the souls of loved ones around them, and perhaps Alice was now thinking of death with at least a bit of hope.

It became clearer to me that this ability to sense souls was a privilege, a privilege given to me by Albert. I felt tremendous gratitude, and also felt more acceptance of his suicide. His death, and the contact he had made with me that first night, had taught me to feel or hear these other messages. I gained a new kind of clarity from the intensity of that night — without it, I wouldn't be able to perceive these other souls. I had received an amazing gift.

In the months that followed, I had more intense psychic encounters. Some of these experiences were emotionally draining. They had a profound effect on me, though I don't believe it's important to write too much about my feelings or reactions to the events. I have no way of knowing the effect of my "psychic readings" on those I was destined to share them with. It is important to describe the events as they happened, and I hope there is a ripple effect in recapitulating them, as there is a ripple effect to our acts of kindness.

When I reflect on my life, I sometimes have the

feeling I've had very bad timing. I've had to work hard for every break I got in life. Surviving AIDS was a major battle. The years that followed Albert's death, however, became increasingly easier, and were possibly the easiest years of my life. Things seemed to flow more smoothly than before. I was always in the right place at exactly the right time. Even business transactions were simpler, and many opportunities have effortlessly come my way since then. I have a sense that, in some way beyond my comprehension, this gentle flow of life may have been guided by Albert.

Several psychic interactions occurred between January 1995 and July 1996. Three of them follow.

In January, for the first time in years, I felt I had put on too much weight, and was getting rather fat. I armed myself with a New Year's resolution to work out regularly. My ambitious goal was to use the Stairmaster equipment for thirty minutes a day, six days a week. I rejoined the Athletic Club, and went in during the afternoons to avoid crowds. I always took along a cassette tape or a good book to alleviate some of the boredom. Even though I had been a bodybuilder, I always disliked exercise.

As I was going through my routine one afternoon, a young man walked in front of me and came over to the drinking fountain next to me. He wasn't particularly interesting, rather plain, yet I felt drawn to him. I had not seen him at the gym before.

I felt a strong connection with Albert, and I sensed another soul around this gentleman. This time, the soul spoke directly to me. It was loud, intense, similar to Albert the night he died. This soul had a four-word message and wanted me to relay it to the stranger.

But I wasn't going to stop in the middle of my workout and relay a message to a stranger — he'd think I was crazy. I continued on the machine for five minutes or so, but Albert kept insisting I stop and deliver that simple four-word message. I ignored Albert and continued my workout.

After about ten minutes, the gentleman passed in front of me again, and our eyes met. He had retrieved his gym bag from the locker room, and was leaving the club. I was torn between telling and not telling. Then the internal debate subsided, and I got off the Stairmaster and reluctantly approached the man. The words came out effortlessly.

"Do you believe in psychic phenomena?" I asked.

"I don't feel strongly either way," he said. As he said it, his "guardian angel" clearly gave me a lot of information, almost instantaneously. He told me that he had died of AIDS, that he had been a television set designer, and that he was small-framed man when he was alive.

"I think we all have some psychic ability," I said. "I have a message to give you from a friend of yours who died. He was a television set designer, a small-framed man. He died of AIDS."

The man froze. Tears came to his eyes.

"That was my lover, Bob.... Yesterday was the one-year anniversary of his death. You don't need to tell me the message. I can tell it to you. Last night I cried myself to sleep. I prayed and cried most of the night. I kept saying, 'Can you hear me, Bob? Can you hear me?'"

We stood and stared at each other.

"Go ahead," he said. "Tell me the message."

I can hear you was the four-word message. We hugged each other, and we both shed tears.

We have run into each other since, and when we do, David always greets me with a huge, warm smile. I was not prepared for experiences with complete strangers, and this was the second time it had happened. It seemed to benefit them in some way, but I wasn't sure how to react or what to do with this gift. And I didn't know anyone else who would be able to answer that question for me.

The incidents could not be forced; I couldn't make them happen, and they didn't happen when expected. They unfolded in their own way, on their own schedule.

Although the episode with David was powerful at

the time, the significance of it faded over the next few days. The next experience, though, was too powerful to ever fade from memory.

During the first few weeks at my new building, I made a point of being as polite as possible to my new neighbors and the building staff. The staff was small, and I knew I would be seeing them daily for a long time to come.

A young Hispanic woman named Carmen worked at the front desk. She seemed to be in a world of her own. She wasn't exactly rude, but she certainly wasn't friendly. She seemed distant towards everyone. Nearly every afternoon I would say hello and pay her some kind of compliment. She seldom responded, but I kept up the effort, week after week. I wasn't quite sure why it seemed so important to make an extra effort, but I did.

As I was leaving the building one afternoon, I passed her desk and complimented her hairstyle and her sweater. Something felt different, though — I sensed the presence of a spirit "talking" to me, trying to communicate. I could sense the message and its words, intensely and clearly. The spirit described herself as she appeared when she was alive, and said she had an urgent message for Carmen.

But I certainly didn't know Carmen very well, and I was afraid to say something like this to her. I worried about my reputation — if I shared these things, everyone in the building, including Carmen, might think I'm a lunatic. People love to gossip in high-rises. It would be fuel for stories that could make living there very uncomfortable.

I left for the library, where I had research to do, but kept feeling the presence of this soul, begging me to return and give Carmen the message. Part of the message was that her sister-in-law was pregnant, and so I decided to simply approach Carmen and ask her if she had a sister-in-law who was pregnant. If she said no, I wouldn't pursue it further. If she said yes, I might find the courage to let the spirit guide me. I canceled my dinner plans and headed back to the building. The lobby was empty, except for Carmen.

"Back already?" she said.

"Yes, I forgot to do something.... By the way, do you have a sister-in-law who's pregnant?"

She pulled her lips together and glared at me with dark eyes. She was disturbed and curious at the same time.

"How the hell do you know?"

I took a long, deep breath. "I had what I guess you'd call a psychic experience. A spirit told me."

"Did someone put you up to this? Is this some- one's idea of a joke? Really, how the hell do you know?"

I described in detail the physical description the

spirit had given me. Carmen identified her as the aunt who had raised her, and who had died a few years before. Carmen was quiet, even somber, and she confessed that her sister-in-law was pregnant, and no one except her knew about it yet. Her sister-in-law had cheated on her husband, and was afraid the baby wasn't his. She had just told Carmen about it the night before, in a private confession. She was sick with worry, and considering an abortion.

I relayed the message: The baby was indeed the child of her husband, Carmen's brother. The woman must not have an abortion. This child was important. The spirit was looking after both Carmen and the baby, and there was no need to worry. Carmen would soon be relieved of the extraordinary anxiety she had been experiencing.

Then the spirit revealed some personal things from Carmen's childhood that I told her about. The information meant little to me, but seemed relevant to her.

Carmen and I enjoyed a fond and friendly relationship after that. She seemed lighter in the days that followed, and I was glad I had shared what I knew with her.

For some time afterward, I questioned this new position of being a messenger. I questioned it logically, and emotionally. I thought about how it felt, physically, to receive these signals. The sensations were very specific. I remembered I had felt them once when I was a child, ten years old, riding a bus. There was a woman on the bus, and this voice — this sensation — told me she was suffering and needed help very badly. I wanted to comfort her but I was forbidden to speak to strangers.

I had a few more of these intuitive promptings, but as I got older I started to question them, and eventually tuned them out altogether. I believe we all have some psychic ability — these experiences certainly couldn't be unique to me. Perhaps the ability to perceive these things is stronger in childhood and, as we age, we lose touch with this ability. The world conditions us not to give any credence to those events.

When I was an underage seventeen-year-old, I went to the dog track with my friend Robert Cohen. I won every bet I placed, four bets on the first day. We went back a second and third day, and I won those bets as well. I can't imagine why I didn't go back again. I was probably afraid my parents would find out what I was up to, and discover my sins. I considered the windfall a streak of good luck. I haven't gambled since then, but I do remember sensing the numbers of the winners come into my head. Those sensations had something in common with what was now happening, though the situation was certainly different.

All these incidents — Carmen, David, Alice, finding Albert's note, his subsequent messages to me — had a similar feeling to them. It felt like being coddled, being embraced in a way. It felt warm physically, and afterward I felt more hopeful. Though I was still apprehensive about discussing these things with others, I was learning to open up to the messages.

Cliff was the one person I was perfectly comfortable sharing these things with, and our friendship continued to grow. We had long and enjoyable conversations about my experiences, and about his fascinating career in photography as well. He continued to help me see my own strength.

In February, Cliff became a witness to another contact with Albert, one that was extraordinary for both of us. We were having lunch at Votre Sante, a restaurant on LaBrea Avenue. He had just photographed Brad Pitt, and I was asking him about that, and about other celebrity photo shoots. He was reluctant to talk much about them, and kept shifting the conversation back to me and my life.

I began to share in detail the psychic experiences I was having, and at that point, I told him I wasn't particularly happy these things were going on. It felt like they had been thrust upon me, and I wasn't quite sure why. Cliff listened enthusiastically, and encouraged me to tell others about it. I wasn't sure if there was value in that. Even now, I have mixed feelings about it all. I don't think it's necessary to know about our futures, for one thing. Life and our individual destinies evolve according to their own plan and at their own pace. But Cliff thought there was a possibility that sharing these events might be important. He said they might be valuable to some other people, and it might be a necessary step in my evolution, as well. I told him I would consider it. Often the words of our friends are messages from the universe.

Toward the end of the meal, I sensed Albert's presence, and also the presence of another soul, who was attempting to impart events that I could actually feel — painful events. It was as if part of me was reliving this person's death. Instinctively, I knew the message was for Cliff and told him what I was feeling. He encouraged me to tell him everything that came up.

I described this person, and for the first time, I referred to Cliff as Clifford. He sat silently, and then he began to get emotional and wanted to leave the restaurant. The experience was intense and I felt somewhat drained by it, so the idea of leaving appealed to me, too.

We walked to Cliff's large, airy apartment and settled into two comfortable chairs. Cliff acknowledged that he knew exactly who I had described and asked me to continue. I sensed the soul again, and heard these words:

Clifford, I love you. Thank you so much for coming. Thank you for being there. I so badly wanted to tell you this then. I needed to tell you this. I waited for you to come. Clifford, I love you, and I will always love you. I am no longer in pain. Thank you for coming.

I was extremely tired. The experience had overwhelmed me. Cliff, on the other hand, seemed relaxed and relieved. He had a client coming soon, and offered me his guest room so I could take a brief nap. I slept for about an hour, and when I woke, the white room was full of sun and I felt refreshed. I could hear Cliff in the other room, still talking with his client. I waited for them to finish, then joined Cliff in his office.

He told me that I had described his friend Al, who had died a few years earlier. I had never met him, and Cliff had never mentioned him. Al was from Northern California, and they had been friends for over fifteen years. Al had contracted AIDS and the virus was particularly virulent. His health deteriorated rapidly. Cliff was working in New York at the time and had gotten word from a mutual friend that Al didn't have much time to live. Cliff rushed from

New York to be by his side.

By the time he arrived, Al had been delirious and was now in a coma. The nurse told Cliff that he had been yelling the name Clifford for two days. Cliff sat with Al for the last few hours of his life, holding hands, and saying his good-byes. Though he mumbled from his coma, Al was unable to communicate.

Cliff told me the description had been completely accurate, and mentioned that the song, "That's What Friends Are For" had been playing in the restaurant when this communication began. It was a song they had shared and referred to often. Cliff had always been a spiritually oriented person, and this experience confirmed beliefs he already held. I had shared Al's last words with him.

For me, the importance of sharing these experiences was becoming clearer, and I began to consider the possibility of committing them to paper.

CHAPTER 8

More Signals

Sometime after the experience with Cliff, I had another encounter that was almost as intense as the first contact from Albert.

One Saturday night, I was invited to a local nightclub to spend a few hours with two friends. But the music was too loud for any meaningful conversation, and I wanted to get away from the noise and darkness. I went to the entrance and started talking to the coat check person. His name was Michael Herbertson, and though we were strangers, I was much more comfortable hanging out with him than inside the club. He seemed distracted, but he welcomed the company, and we sat in the little room, not much bigger than a closet.

Michael began to tell me about a dysfunctional relationship he was in, and then I clearly sensed Albert's presence once again. At the same time, I felt the presence of Michael's mother and sensed she had just recently died. Her presence was very definite and — unlike my experience with Carmen, Cliff, and David — she was communicating a message specifically for me, as well as one for Michael.

I was hesitant; I did not want to scare Michael. I asked him if he had an opinion about psychic phenomena, and he said he was very open to the possibility. When I nervously asked if his mother had recently died, he teared up instantly, and I felt apprehensive about saying more. She had died just two days before.

He seemed to be receptive, and I knew he needed the message, so I went on to tell him about the experiences I'd had. I told him they had begun after Albert's death, that I was not by any means a professional psychic, and that I actually had very little experience with these things. I told him that I had sensed souls around others, and that it seemed like they were guardian angels for them. I said that sometimes I was simply aware of them, and other times they communicated with me. I told him I sensed his mother in this way.

"Please, tell me what she wants to say," he said. So I began.

Michael, it's Mom. I love you very much. I know how much you loved me. There is no need to tell me. I know how badly you wanted to say good-bye and hold me. I am always with you. Forgive your stepfather for not telling you I was dying. Forgive him for not sharing my possessions with you. I know you wanted something of mine to hold on to. But I am always with you. I will always be looking out for you. I love you, my baby. In your heart is where you will find me. I have never left you. I will be near you through your entire life. I will be your light in darkness.

Michael and I sat silently among the coats for a few moments in our own little world. His face was soft, his cheeks wet with tears.

Quickly and briefly, she spoke again — this time to me.

Joel, we're no more separate from our off-spring than we are from each and every human being. Some of us struggle to teach our children the lessons we have learned in our own lifetimes. We fear we will be separated from them at death. We want so badly to give them what we haven't had, and to share with them what we've learned. Individuals will not be separated from their children. Their paths will cross again and again. These relationships are infinite. They are bound to each other, and will repeat these relationships in different roles.

You will tell others what you are now learning. Some you will reach, and in turn they will reach others. It is these small steps that will bring all of us to a higher consciousness. From where you stand, it appears this evolution is slow. It is unfolding. The fact that you now can see this unfolding is a gift. Those that see this within their own lifetime have been given a great gift. This gift is from the suffering, and the work in the past. This greater good is unfolding over many lifetimes.

Then she spoke to Michael again.

Michael, along the way, I will signal you again.

Michael said, "What if I don't recognize you?"

Then I will signal you again. Look inside yourself for answers.

And then they were gone. We were quiet for a while, and then we hugged. Both of us were crying. It must have been a funny sight for the patrons passing by — Michael is six foot five inches, and I'm five foot six.

Michael told me his mother had died of cancer and his stepfather didn't let him know when she was in her final days. His stepfather had sold most of his mother's possessions shortly before her death, and Michael had nothing tangible to remember her by.

He was thrilled by the encounter, and so was I. We were energized. I've run into him half a dozen times since that night, and we feel a bond because of that experience. He's had many successes in his life since then. He's become a successful nightclub promoter and screenwriter. He's in a healthy relationship. Each time we have met, he has told me that he feels very blessed, and knows that he is being guided from beyond, just as he was guided by her love when she was alive. He told me she has signaled him many times over the years, and that night at the club had completely transformed a painful event into a beautiful experience.

Right after that experience with Michael, at the insistence of Ed Foley and Sharon, I began keeping a journal. I began sharing these stories with others as well.

In March of 1995, I ran into an old acquaintance, Mark Hines, at the gym. He was warm and sympathetic, and told me that I looked in better health, and that I didn't look quite as sad as I had before. He apologized for not knowing what to say when he had heard about Albert's suicide; he said I looked so distraught that he couldn't find the words to comfort me. He said he knew how close Albert and I had been. I was grateful for his warm greeting and the acknowledgment of my loss. It felt to me that people seemed to support my grieving for a few months, and then their support began to fade. The losses we experience can be much deeper and last much longer than the support friends and family can provide. It can be especially helpful to receive this kind of support long after the loss has occurred. I was grateful for his simple act of kindness.

I thanked Mark for being so thoughtful to mention these things so many months after Albert's death. We said good-bye, and I returned to my workout. Moments later, I felt the presence of a spirit once again, one that wanted to communicate with Mark. And there was a second, distinct spirit. One was that of an old woman, the other was a young girl.

I knew instantly that the girl was four years old and had died in an accident. I thought something she had to say might be a source of comfort for Mark, so I went and found him, and asked if we could speak privately in the cafe.

I told him I had been experiencing some unusual things since Albert's death, and I asked if he believed in the possibility of having an encounter with someone's spirit after they had died. He said absolutely not — he was a Catholic and this was definitely not part of his belief system. I only half listened to his answer, though, and proceeded with careless enthusiasm to tell him that I could feel two spirits watching over him — one an older woman, perhaps his grandmother, the other a four-year-old child who had died in an accident.

Mark was very quiet, and then told me that his baby sister had died in a car accident at four years old. He regarded me with a cold distrust — not what I expected. I mumbled a few things about the fact that they would always be with him. I told him his sister was safe and with his grandmother. It was obvious Mark wanted to end the discussion. In the months that followed, he kept his distance.

I learned something else about these encounters: perhaps it isn't always necessary to share them. In some cases, it may be better not to.

I had several similar experiences in the months that followed. I shared them with only three people, and was apprehensive each time. But those three people were pleased that I did.

A few years before Albert's death, I was interviewed for a BBC film. An acquaintance and neighbor, Dr. Simon Levey, was a scientist who had received quite a bit of attention for his work on the genetics of human sexuality. When he asked for a handful of volunteers willing to be interviewed about growing up gay, I gladly accepted the opportunity. The film eventually aired on PBS, and Simon got a call from a friend of his who had seen me in the film. He wanted to meet me, and asked Simon to set up a blind date. Simon seemed to think the chemistry between us might be good. His name was Xavier Carrica.

We went out to dinner, and I enjoyed his company, but, for several reasons, I knew the relationship would never evolve into more than a friendship. We certainly didn't dislike each other, we were just very different people. I welcomed a new friend, though. We had three more dates over a month's time, then it dwindled to occasional contact. In March of 1995, I ran into him at Pavillions grocery store. We caught up on events in our lives, but I didn't mention any of my recent psychic episodes with him. We exchanged phone numbers and made plans to work out together the following week.

Later that night, just as I was drifting off to sleep, I sensed the presence of yet another soul. This was the first time I had felt a presence other than Albert when I was alone. It was Xavier's grandmother. She flashed an almost perfect photographic image of herself into my mind's eye. She was wearing a black and white dress with a cross-stitched flower pattern. Her sleeves were pulled up high, and she had eight clips on her sleeves. She wore flat open-toe shoes, and had extremely long black hair, speckled with gray and pulled into a bun.

I was so excited that I got up and called Xavier. I explained I'd been having unique experiences since Albert's death, and told him about what had been happening. He seemed receptive, so I asked about his grandmother, and gave him a description of her. He giggled — he was delighted to hear it. She had been wearing that dress the last time he saw her. She was a hairdresser and always had hair clips attached to her sleeves. He confirmed that everything in my description was accurate.

There had been no message, but I told him that I assumed she wanted him to know she was with him and watched over him. Whenever I ran into him after that, he would ask if I had a message from his grandmother. I didn't, although I wished I did. I suggested that he try to stay open to her presence and one day she might signal him. So far, it hasn't happened.

I never cared for or believed in astrology, numerology, tarot, or any other attempts at predicting our futures. The events as I've described them have affected my sense of spirituality as much as the new AIDS drugs have affected my health. When people ask my opinion about professional psychics, I try to avoid giving an opinion. I can't speak for anyone else, but I believe that each and every one of us has the ability to communicate with deceased loved ones. I believe drugs, alcohol, caffeine, stress, and other distractions from this existence inhibit that ability. When we are in a relaxed state, similar to a peaceful awakening from sleep or coming out of meditation, all of us can connect with our departed loved ones. They are always listening. They can and will answer us. Their voices can be very quiet. Rather than seeking validation from outside sources, we have to believe and trust in the love we have already shared.

All of the messages or signals from Albert that I've described were of an intimate and serious nature. They weren't imparted for entertainment. And they weren't something I had control over. If I had a choice, I might choose to avoid the encounters, but having experienced them, I can't call them good or bad, positive or negative.

Obviously, it's easier and more enjoyable to experience life in good health. Financial security lends a certain stability to one's life. The warmth and comfort of friends definitely soothes the inevitable bumps in life's rocky road. But even without these things, I've acquired a profound belief that, as Albert's first message to me relayed,

All of life's moments have meaning and purpose and are connected to a greater good.

This keeps me from making quick judgments. Things are not always as they appear. Suffering and pain today may bring vast, beneficial changes tomorrow.

I now believe our species is evolving in a positive direction. I believe we are slowly moving toward a "collective consciousness." I believe most human beings are inherently good. I believe each and every one of us can effect positive change in the universe, and we effect that change by even the smallest acts of kindness.

Albert's messages were all different. Some were more profound than others. Some were long, others brief. Some happened alone, others were witnessed by friends. The experiences always reminded me of life's unexpected changes. Life will ebb and flow in its own direction and on its own schedule.

There will be pain and suffering for all of us. We have a choice in how we perceive it. There will be moments of joy and laughter and love. It seems wise to look upon the pleasant moments of life during the trying times. It seems our best choice of perception. Everything in life will pass. No trouble will last forever. Perhaps it is the indescribable thing we call love that paves our way. I cannot imagine this journey without it.

CHAPTER 9

Signals for New Friends

To this day, Albert continues to signal me. I am always glad when these events take place, but I am most happy when they occur in the presence of other people, as they often do.

Not long ago, I was consoling a new friend named Eddie Auger, who was distraught over — what else? — love issues. As we spoke, a tiny hummingbird flew into my home and landed directly on my shoulder. The little bird allowed me to touch it and pet it, and I cupped it in my hands and passed it to Eddie. He didn't quite know what to make of it. He assumed the bird was ill. I told him to walk out on the balcony and release the bird. The moment he got outside, the bird flew away, obviously in good health.

Eddie was delighted. He told me that he had prayed for help and for a signal that very morning. It was an honor to share this small miracle with Eddie.

A bit later, I was speaking to a neighbor, a kind and wonderful woman named Lori Loughlin. She was an actress on the television show *Full House*. She had married the clothing designer Mossimo and was pregnant at the time. While I was with her, I could feel a soul telling me she would have some minor complications with the birth, but everything would be okay. I told her that I sensed the baby would arrive a bit earlier than expected; it was due on September 17th. She asked me how I knew this. I simply told her I sensed it.

Lori went into labor on September 16th, and her doctors had to perform a cesarean section. Hence, the baby came into the world that afternoon — just a bit early.

It has been almost four years since I first began to document these experiences. While I wrote this book, I had many distractions. The largest was buying and remodeling a home in L.A. After I completed that task, I had a housewarming party. A friend brought along a location agent. I learned that, in L.A., even houses have agents. If your house has the right qualities, it can be used in TV, film, or print work. The agent convinced me to list my new home with her agency. Right away, my house was getting work — and this new venture was lucrative.

One day I was working out at Gold's Gym in

Hollywood and a young fashion designer approached me. His name was Anthony Franco. He had seen the house in a magazine and admired it. He needed to use a large house for a fashion shoot, but was just getting started in his career and didn't have a lot of money to spend. He couldn't afford to book the house through the location agent. He was very flattering and really wanted to use my house, so I offered it to him no charge.

The shoot was to begin at 10 A.M. At 9 A.M., my doorbell rang, and there stood a radiant, beautiful young woman. At first glance I assumed she was one of the models showing up early. I opened the door and she wrapped her arms around me and gave me an overwhelmingly enthusiastic hug.

She blurted out, "Joel, I am so glad to have found you after ten years. Now I can thank you."

It was an intense greeting for 9 A.M., and an awkward moment for me. Something in her eyes was familiar, but I couldn't quite remember where I knew her from. Her next words were no help.

She said, "I'm Natalie Raitano," and cracked an unusually stunning smile. "As soon as I heard that Anthony was shooting at Joel Rothschild's house, I had to come and see you. I owe you so much. Thanks."

After another awkward moment, I remembered: She was a very young girl who had worked at

Portofino Tanning Salon. I had used the salon for one month in 1990. Now I had placed her face, but I still had no idea why she was so enthusiastic.

"You don't remember me?" she asked.

I said, "Yes, you're the girl from the tanning salon."

"But you don't understand why I'm so grateful," she said. She explained, and then I remembered.

The tanning salon was in Beverly Hills and catered to a very snotty crowd. On Natalie's second day at work there, a Hollywood celebrity came in to use one of the tanning beds. When I came in, Natalie was at the front desk struggling to get the computer operational. The celebrity came out of the room at that moment and berated Natalie — in a nasty, condescending, and mean-spirited way — for not being more proficient at her job. I have always taken exception to such behavior, and I told off the celebrity, suggesting that she treat all people with the same respect that she demands.

Natalie was very grateful, and we spoke often during the next few weeks. She was pursuing a career in acting and had been feeling discouraged. I told her she was exceptionally beautiful and, even more important, had a very kind nature. I was certain that, if she could act, she would find work. I encouraged her to follow her dreams.

Now, so many years later, Natalie told me she had found those simple words inspirational. She had followed her dreams. She is now working as a lead character in the very successful syndicated TV show, *VIP,* with Pamela Anderson.

During this reunion, I began to sense two spirits around Natalie. One was a younger man, the other an older woman. Both wanted to communicate messages to her, but I hesitated to mention it at the time. The photographers, models, and stylists had all arrived, and the energy was high and wild. I told Natalie that I appreciated her memories, and that the story reminded me again that even small acts of kindness can have a ripple effect. We hugged good-bye and I headed into my office.

Several weeks later, Natalie called again, just to say hello. I was working on this book and told her what I was writing. She said she very badly wanted to read the manuscript. I was hesitant because it was a very rough first draft, but I reluctantly sent her a copy. The next day she called and told me how much she enjoyed the book, and we made arrangements to have lunch the following day.

During lunch, she was incredibly encouraging — she gave me exactly the same kind of support I'd given her years earlier. I felt comfortable, at ease with her, and I told her I had sensed two spirits around her before, and now I was sensing them again. Natalie was excited and receptive to any messages they had for her.

I described the spirits in detail. I asked her not to tell me anything about these people, only to tell me if my description was accurate with a simple yes or no. She smiled her disarming smile and nodded yes. I knew the message was correct. For the next fifty minutes, I relayed a detailed personal message to Natalie. When I finished, she was overwhelmed, and we both cried. That day we forged a bond of friendship that continues even now.

CHAPTER 10

Conclusion, Signal

August 1998

These signs, signals, messages, and events continue to enrich my life. I am grateful for them in many ways, on many levels.

Time and time again I have pondered these events. I have debated, within myself and with many others, about these experiences. Even though I lived through them firsthand, I have questioned them.

I am by nature a skeptic, and so are most of the people I have known. It is quite logical to be one. We live in this physical world, a realm we learn to navigate equipped with only our five senses. We grow through our concrete experiences. It seems reasonable to believe that when a body dies, it is the end of life as we know it. Even if you believe in one of the world's religions, life beyond death is something vastly different from anything we can conceive.

When loved ones are taken from our lives, it seems comforting for some of us to cling to the notion we will see them again, especially when the pain and loss are recent and fresh. Perhaps it is human vanity that plants the seed of eternal hope that we will go on after death. Human beings certainly are vain creatures. But perhaps it is the stronger emotion of love that allows us, and shows us how, to believe in a hereafter, in another world not unlike this one, only different in ways we cannot imagine.

Whatever the reasons we choose to believe in life after death, we do so with faith and hope.

But a good skeptic can come up with an unlimited supply of explanations for stories like mine. The most reasonable is that the writer concocted the whole story for personal gain. And these psychic experiences all lack credible scientific documentation. Within the confines of our physical world, they lack the reproducibility and tangibility that we require. Anyone who believes in these stories has made some kind of leap of faith, or else has an innate desire to believe in something greater than our senses can fathom and absorb. Believing these stories to be true opens one to a litany of logical and unanswerable questions.

It seems easiest to discount the story. Even a hopeful optimist might choose to dismiss these stories, to put them in the file in his or her memory bank labeled uncertain or dubious. The signals have been so subtle that they could easily have been purely imaginary. They always seem to tell us to have hope, without telling us why. We cannot live on hope alone. Hope does not take pain away. Hope does not bring our loved ones back to life as we knew them.

Hope, however, is what keeps some of us alive. An infinitely small bit of hope is what kept me clinging and fighting for my life during my most serious illness in 1994. Lack of hope certainly played a part in Albert's suicide, and in the deaths of so many others we have known. Hope is very real within me.

I did not fabricate any of this book. I wrote it with the sincerest of beliefs that the hope it contains may help others. With each of these experiences, my faith has grown stronger. I am, however, a physical being, and bound to the physical world. It is impossible for me (at least, with my current belief system) to live twenty-four hours a day, seven days a week in a state of hope, faith, or optimism. It is impossible for me to constantly focus on the bigger picture I believe to be true. I can lose sight of many of the lessons I have learned, lessons that have enlightened my being and soul.

Sometimes a new incident or an old memory reminds me of what I have learned. Sometimes friends remind me. I'm a very busy person, far too much of the time. Maybe later on in life I'll gain enough wisdom to slow down and simplify my life. I spend a lot of time tending to life's pressures, needs, and responsibilities. Even a simple hobby like gardening turns into a major project that keeps me dutifully focused on this world. Often I lose sight of my own spiritual beliefs. I lose contact with my faith. Life has a way of distracting us from our spiritual lessons — yet, if I totally accept Albert's words on the night he died, then even the distracted moments matter, and are just as important as any other moments.

Midway through writing this book, something strange happened that I believe was another signal from Albert. Yet it was vastly different from any others. I still suffer with AIDS neuropathy in my feet and hands, a side effect that makes writing especially difficult, and my handwriting looks like a child's chicken scratches. I didn't know how to type and was computer illiterate when I began this book, but I eventually went out and bought a computer with voice-activated software. To my complete amazement, I learned to work with a laptop computer and the dictation software.

My life was quite full. I was very busy writing and also had a larger number of responsibilities than usual to deal with involving health, relationships, and family. When all these things converged, I was completely distracted, and I lost contact with my spiritual side, and with thoughts of Albert, too. I managed to give a few hours to writing each day, transcribing my thoughts, then backing up the text to a disk and printing out a copy.

At the time, I had been living with my former partner, Keith, for almost two years. He worked in a laboratory as a microbiologist. I was writing when he came home one evening, and he reminded me that we had to pick up my parents soon for dinner. I quickly ended the dictation, backed up the text, and began to print. I was trying to hurry, and wasn't thinking about the content of this book, or Albert, or spirituality of any kind. One by one, the pages of the chapter came out of the printer, and then another page came out, after the chapter had ended. It was nearly blank, except for a tiny heart, in the topmost corner of the paper, way outside the normal margins.

This little oddity may have been dismissed and forgotten by many people, but given what had happened, it caught my attention. Keith was bewildered too. I hadn't added it to the text, and we hadn't seen this heart on anything else. I checked the new box of paper I'd put in the printer, looking for another heart. Each sheet was perfectly blank. I pondered the heart and searched for a logical explanation.

Later that evening, I showed the heart to Ed

Foley, who happened to be the only person who had ever seen Albert's final note back in 1994. He reminded me that Albert had drawn a tiny heart on his note. I remembered that little heart, and made a connection. I believe this was a physical signal for me from Albert.

The little heart has popped up seven or eight times since then — always in the corner, way beyond the margins. It has happened on two different computers, with two different printers. The symbol is nowhere that I know of on the software. I wouldn't know how to print one out if I tried. I've copied it and printed it to scale on the last page of this book. Ponder it if you like; it's quite an amazing "coincidence" that this little heart, so like Albert's on his note, suddenly appears without cause.

I choose to believe it's another signal — granted, many might not, but I certainly can't see any logical explanation for it. I believe the little heart, with love, crossed from beyond our world.

Albert and I shared a deep friendship during a war. We had profound admiration and respect for each other. The day he took his own life was the most painful day of my life. That great loss drastically altered the course of my life — yet it provided me with miracles that I could never have conceived possible.

All of my fellow comrades lost their battles against AIDS. Many of them left me with wonderful memories. Albert alone left me with a gift.

Perhaps somehow he realized after his death how much additional pain he created for me. Maybe that is the reason why he has contacted me so many times. I still have questions that remain unanswered. Even for me, doubt creeps in. But after the moments of internal debate, I remember Albert's words to me, in those precious moments in time, and I remember when the heart appeared, and I am filled with the gift of hope.

That hope brings a smile to my face. That hope is something real that will light my way in the dark moments. And when it is my time to die, I will go forward with that hope, with faith and a smile, without fear, remembering the little heart, and all of Albert's signals.

I would like to think that, as a result of reading this, some of you — the more open-minded ones, the less skeptical ones — might have an awakening of some kind, and become aware of our connection to a far greater world, a far greater reality. I would like to think that some of you might become more aware and receptive to the signals that departed loved ones may be sending you. There could be tremendous healing and love in those messages.

By reading this story, you have also fulfilled Albert's final wish not to be forgotten. Thank you.

A Last-Minute Epilog

September 3, 1999

It has been a year since that little heart popped up on my printer, and I have gone from computer illiterate to surfing the net. During those twelve months, contacts with Albert have been less frequent but not insignificant. I still deeply miss my old friends, but my relationships with Natalie Raitano, Ed Auger, Cliff Watts, and other new friends have deepened.

My garden has blossomed, and I am feeding a group of raccoons that live in the brush. More gray hair has popped up on my head, and with a few exceptions my health has been steady during these twelve months. Keith's research has been published in two scientific journals. I have a new Jack Russell terrier named Billy. Keith named him after William Shakespeare. He loves to taunt the small family of hummingbirds that has nested in the morning glory vines.

Once I had completed a final draft of this manu-

Once I had completed a final draft of this manuscript, I began to share copies with my family and friends, and then I sent a few off to some writers. One of those was Neale Donald Walsch. He gave the manuscript to his assistant, Cathy Bolton, to review. She resonated with my story, and told me that she was in tears when she read the first chapter. I called her and we had a wonderful conversation. She told me she had always loved hummingbirds, and that she fed them in the summer and watched for their return each spring. She is a singer, and her latest album is called *Wind Beneath My Wings.*

She sent me a copy of her album, and I listened to her beautiful voice and enjoyed her version of the song. Another song on her album happened to be my childhood favorite, and on the CD jacket insert, some time before, she had placed a little heart, exactly like the ones Albert had sent to me. Cathy and I discussed these odd little coincidences, and we instantly felt a warm bond of friendship. She had told Mr. Walsch about my book, but he was busy and hadn't read it.

My ego wanted his support, yet we both agreed to leave it to fate and I surrendered it to the universe. A few days later, as she was printing out a report for him, an extra blank page came through the printer with four little hearts, exactly like the ones I had been getting on my printer. She was delighted, and called and told me about them. I felt the four hearts were a sign, and that one was for Albert and the other three represented Cathy and her two children.

The next morning, she showed the little hearts to Mr. Walsch. He and his wife Nancy were getting ready for a trip to Korea and Europe. He told Cathy to pack my manuscript in with a few other things for him to read.

Weeks passed, and I didn't hear from Mr. Walsch. Then late last night my dog Billy woke me from a deep sleep with a faint cry. I got up and decided to check my e-mail, and there was his foreword. It was so beautiful I was filled with tears. And I knew his kind words would carry my story to many more people.

Then I realized another "coincidence" had occurred: I treasure a work of art that hangs across from my bed. It is the last thing Albert and I ever purchased together, a valuable engraving by a famous eighteenth-century Italian artist, Guisseppe Vasi. A few weeks before Albert died, I dragged him to a thrift store and we found it for just $100. I have looked at it every day since then, and it has become Keith's favorite thing in our home. I had thought the miracle was finding something so beautiful for so little money. I was wrong. It is a view from the Fiume Arno, near where Neale Donald Walsch was standing when he felt inspired to write my foreword.

Now when I pray, I often ask that those of you

who have taken my book to heart and those of you who have experienced your own signals will spread the word. There is a spiritual awakening taking place on our small blue planet, and it is the greatest gift we have been given. I believe those who have experienced this gift have an obligation to hold out hope for those who have not yet seen it.

These kind of events, in my life and yours, are not accidents or mere coincidences. They are things that are affecting our entire collective consciousness, and have the power to create a better life, and a better world, for us all. I pray that you will go forth and carry the messages of love, kindness, and hope to others.

In Loving Memory of Albert Fleites

October 5, 1961–June 1, 1994

'Tis not the many oaths that make the truth,
But the plain single vow that vow'd true.

— William Shakespeare
All's Well That Ends Well

About the Author

Joel Rothschild is a long-term AIDS survivor. He was born and raised in Miami Beach, Florida. After graduating from Florida Atlantic University he pursued his hobby of bodybuilding and opened a health spa in Atlanta, Georgia. It was an immediate success, and attracted celebrities such as Arnold Schwartzenegger and Bruce Springsteen. After a few years in Atlanta he moved to Los Angeles, where he has lived ever since, outliving his doctors' prognosis for death (and outliving two of his doctors). He has worked as an AIDS activist, and he volunteers and supports several charities. His hobbies include gardening, working out, and writing poetry.

Speaking Engagements and Consultations

Joel Rothschild is available on a limited basis for speaking engagements and seminars. Every effort will be made to accommodate those that benefit charitable organizations.

On a case-by-case basis, he will meet with those seeking his intuitive or psychic abilities. He does not accept payment for these services. In lieu of payment a donation made to either a cancer, AIDS, or children's charity is required.

To contact Mr. Rothschild please write to:

P.O. Box 38773
Los Angeles, CA 90038 USA
E-mail: Abook4all@AOL.com
Website: www.joelrothschild.com

New World Library publishes books and other
forms of communication on the leading edge
of personal and planetary evolution.

Our books, audio, and video cassettes
are in bookstores everywhere.
For a catalog of our complete library
of publications, contact:

New World Library
14 Pamaron Way
Novato, CA 94949

Telephone: (415) 884-2100
Fax: (415) 884-2199
Toll free: (800) 972-6657
Catalog requests: Ext. 50
Ordering: Ext. 52

E-mail: escort@nwlib.com
http://www.nwlib.com